Praise for
UnCommon Learning

"Too often, school improvement initiatives layer activities upon cultures and systems that are not ready to receive them. UnCommon Learning *rejects the notion that something must be done in addition, and instead begins with changing the foundational culture of a school—consistent with NASSP's Breaking Ranks Framework for School Improvement. Countless schools—and more important, countless students—will no doubt benefit from the guidance Eric shares."*

—JoAnn Bartoletti
Executive Director, National Association of
Secondary School Principals

"In Digital Leadership, *Eric Sheninger trailblazed the path many educational leaders followed to become digitally connected and now, in* UnCommon Learning, *he gets right to the heart of exactly what we need to do to create schools designed to empower today's students. Eric doesn't just talk about change; he has actually led change in his system, and his story is both inspirational and filled with practical tips for implementation."*

—Dave Burgess
New York Times best-selling author of *Teach Like a PIRATE*
and co-author of *P is for Pirate: Inspirational ABC's for Educators*

"Eric's vision and collection of resources to create a student-centered learning experience for schools is something that all educators should read. Although he shares great ideas on what opportunities could look like, he challenges us to push our own thinking of what school could really look like and move forward to become the innovative educators our students need."

—George Couros
Innovative teaching, learning, and leadership consultant

"For the past several years, Eric's mission has been to find effective ways to use technology to improve student performance. In UnCommon Learning: Creating Schools That Work for Kids *he shares the most impactful practices he has found. These practices provide a guide to move school reform, using technology, from a concept to a reality."*

—Dr. Bill Daggett
Chairman and founder, International Center
for Leadership in Education

"UnCommon Learning *is a book that is long overdue! In this most important book for educators at all levels, Eric Sheninger has put into writing what he has 'preached' all over the country for years—that in order to effectively maximize student learning, the technology that is all around us cannot be ignored but instead must be incorporated into the classroom learning process.* UnCommon Learning *will prove to be a game-changer for how we educate children!"*

—**Baruti Kafele**
Principal, education consultant, speaker, and author

"There is a growing movement in this country and others to use what we have learned over the decades about effective teaching and learning to design the next generation of classrooms and schools. Eric Sheninger's new book is a welcome addition that movement. He adeptly walks the line between practical strategies and motivating visions of the near and distant future."

—**Robert J. Marzano**
CEO, Marzano Research

"In this urgent and practical book, Eric Sheninger argues that technology must become as central to students' learning as it is in the 'real' world. UnCommon Learning *will teach educational leaders how to integrate technology into the classroom in ways that reflect today's complex, feedback-rich digital environment."*

—**Daniel H. Pink**
Author of *Drive* and *A Whole New Mind*

"Sheninger, in UnCommon Learning, *identifies key areas for growth within our current school systems. Most importantly, he lays out a simple and intentional path to addressing these areas with the goal of improving learning and the overall school experience for students. Educators, regardless of their role within a school, can use this text as a guide to create optimal learning environments for their students with the ultimate goal of creating schools that provide current, relevant and engaging learning experiences."*

—**Josh Stumpenhorst (@stumpteacher)**
Award-winning teacher and author of *The New Teacher Revolution*

"Unlike so many experts offering prescriptions for our beleaguered schools, Eric Sheninger has walked the walk, running an actual school and striving each day to make it better. In UnCommon Learning, *his ideas, born out of real experience, not wishful thinking, will resonate with smart educators who have seen the Next Big Thing come and go with little to show. Our kids deserve to be surrounded by educators like Sheninger who are willing to examine their own prejudices and practices, then think long and hard about what needs to change."*

—**Greg Toppo**
National education writer and
author of *The Game Believes in You:
How Digital Play Can Make Our Kids Smarter*

UnCommon
Learning

To my incredible wife, Melissa, and kids, Nicholas and Isabella. You all are the foundation that allows me to transform dreams into reality.

UnCommon Learning

Creating Schools That Work for Kids

Eric C. Sheninger

A Joint Publication

FOR INFORMATION:

Corwin

A SAGE Company

2455 Teller Road

Thousand Oaks, California 91320

(800) 233-9936

www.corwin.com

SAGE Publications Ltd.

1 Oliver's Yard

55 City Road

London EC1Y 1SP

United Kingdom

SAGE Publications India Pvt. Ltd.

B 1/I 1 Mohan Cooperative Industrial Area

Mathura Road, New Delhi 110 044

India

SAGE Publications Asia-Pacific Pte. Ltd.

3 Church Street

#10-04 Samsung Hub

Singapore 049483

Executive Editor: Arnis Burvikovs

Associate Editor: Ariel Price

Editorial Assistant: Andrew Olson

Production Editor: Amy Schroller

Copy Editor: Pam Schroeder

Typesetter: C&M Digitals (P) Ltd.

Proofreader: Catherine Forrest

Indexer: Judy Hunt

Cover Designer: Candice Harman

Marketing Manager: Stephanie Trkay

Printed in the United States of America

ISBN 978-1-4833-6575-6

This book is printed on acid-free paper.

Certified Chain of Custody
SUSTAINABLE Promoting Sustainable Forestry
FORESTRY www.sfiprogram.org
INITIATIVE SFI-01268

SFI label applies to text stock

16 17 18 19 10 9 8 7 6 5 4 3 2

ontents

Appendixes

Preface

The world today is changing at a fast pace. We are seeing technology advance at a frenetic rate, which is having a powerful impact on our learners. It is not that our students are actually learning differently per se, but the environment in which they are learning is dramatically different. The engaging aspects of technology today and ubiquitous access to information provide constant engagement to learners of all ages. They have embraced this digital world as it provides consistent relevance and meaning through an array of interactive experiences. As a result the job of schools and educators has become exponentially more difficult as a natural disconnect results when students enter their school buildings. This disconnect manifests itself as the school environment is the exact opposite of this engaging world that our learners are now a part of. If students cannot learn the way we now teach or in the conditions that are prevalent, maybe we need to teach the way they learn and create a school environment that more closely aligns with their world.

This book, *UnCommon Learning*, provides a process for schools to initiate sustainable change resulting in a transformation of the learning culture to one that works better and resonates with our students. It lays out the elements necessary for establishing innovative initiatives that will enhance learning while increasing relevance to personalize both the school and learning experience for all students. Uncommon learning refers to initiatives and pedagogical techniques that are not present in scale in a typical school. If present they are more likely to be isolated practices that have not become systematically embedded as part of school or district culture. These initiatives allow students to use real-world tools to do real-world work, focus on developing skill sets that society demands, respond to student interests, empower students to be owners of their learning, and focus on ways to create an environment that is more reflective of the current digital worlds. They take advantage of an emphasis on deeper learning that new national and state standards provide while allowing students to demonstrate mastery in ways that not only prove attainment but also afford them the ability to acquire and apply skill sets necessary in today's digital worlds. New standards are not seen as impediments but rather opportunities for students to demonstrate conceptual mastery in more authentic ways. The author presents successful uncommon learning initiatives that he helped implement as a school principal as well as examples from other schools across the country. He also pulls on leadership strategies presented in the best-selling book *Digital Leadership: Changing Paradigms for Changing Times* (2014) published by Corwin Press.

Within a framework of uncommon learning initiatives, this book focuses on four key areas that are embedded within each chapter:

- Culture
- Relevance
- Personalization
- Sustainability

Culture trumps strategy. Without the right culture in place it is difficult, if not impossible, to implement school or district initiatives at scale that personalize and individualize the learning experience for students while imparting relevance in the process. A culture needs to be built first where an initial shared vision is created around these focus areas. This book will assist you in developing not only a vision but also a specific plan for action that when implemented and subsequently monitored, will lead to the proliferation of uncommon learning practices.

AUDIENCE

This book should be read by anyone looking to initiate sustainable change system-wide to create schools that work better for our students through the implementation of uncommon learning initiatives. The unique nature of this book is that it caters to a diverse audience as it addresses aspects of innovative learning ideas and initiatives that are cost-effective and scalable. The primary audience for the book is school (superintendents, principals, assistant principals, directors of curriculum, and supervisors) and teacher leaders. A secondary audience is higher education professionals as they could integrate this book into their preparation programs; many people would agree that exposure to unique learning opportunities at that level is limited at best.

THE CALL

For many years New Milford High School was just like virtually every other public school in the United States, defined solely by traditional indicators of success such as standardized test scores, graduation rates, and acceptances to four-year colleges. These indicators have become so embedded in the minds of those judging our schools and work that we, like everyone else, worked hard to focus only on initiatives that would hopefully produce favorable outcomes in those areas. If we were doing well we continued down the same path, allowing the status quo to remain embedded. The mentality of "if it isn't broken, don't fix it" resonated so profoundly with us that we would not have even considered changing our ways. If results were not what our stakeholders wanted, we would hold meetings leading to the development of action plans to get us back on course.

There is still an innate desire to sustain a school structure and function that has remained relatively unchanged for well over a hundred years. This is a problem. We were in a rut and didn't even know it. Luckily change came in the form of a little blue bird that gave me the kick in the butt that I desperately needed back in 2009. Being blessed with an amazing staff, student body, administrative team, and community provided the necessary support needed to move us forward.

This is where I experienced a change in mind-set, which up until this point could best be described as fixed. Carol Dweck (2006) spent decades researching achievement and success, which focused one's mind-set. She found that people who had fixed mind-sets believed that their basic qualities, such as intelligence or talent, were simply fixed traits. As a result they spent time documenting their intelligence or talent instead of developing it. People possessing fixed mind-sets also believed that talent alone creates success without much effort. Dweck's research proved this to not be the case. On the other hand she found that people possessing growth mind-sets believed that their most basic abilities could be developed through dedication and hard work, with their brains and talent as starting points. From this perspective a love of learning and resilience essential for success leads to accomplishment. As Dweck found, all great people have these qualities and can overcome a fixed mentality through choice and motivation.

Moving from a fixed to a growth mind-set and feeding off the daily inspiration that connected learning provides gave me the fuel to create a shared vision that eventually became a reality as a result of action. I was exposed to a whole new world that, until this point, I didn't know existed. Social media provided a doorway to this world where I saw firsthand schools and educators implementing uncommon learning initiatives that were accompanied with results. The problem was that we were not doing anything remotely close to what I experienced through social media. It was at this moment in time that I decided to induce the change that I wished to see in my school and begin down a new path.

For change to be successful, it must be sustained. As educators we must not only be willing to see the process through, but we must also create conditions that promote a change in mentality. Educators need to understand why change is needed and be provided with a clear focus for implementation. If they are then put in a position to take calculated risks, knowing that the support to do so is there, then with each resulting success, an inherent appreciation and value for the change evolve. The change process then gets a boost from an intrinsic motivational force that not only jump-starts the initiative but allows for the embrace of change as opposed to always spending precious time to get staff to buy in to change initiatives. We should never have to sell people on better ways to do our noble work nor rely on mandates and directives. These traditional pathways used to drive change typically result in resentment, undermining, and failure.

Even in the face of challenges in the form of education reform mandates, Common Core alignment, Partnership for Assessment of Readiness for College and Careers (PARCC) exams, new educator evaluation systems, loss of funding, and an aging infrastructure, educators have not only persevered but also proved that positive change can happen with the right mind-set. During a five-year stretch from 2009 through 2014, we saw improvements in the traditional indicators of success by mainly focusing on creating a school that worked better for our students as opposed to one that has always worked well for us as adults. This book will lay out the strategies we implemented in addition to examples from other innovative schools and educators to create a culture focused on uncommon learning initiatives.

CENTRAL FOCUS OF THIS BOOK

The premise of this book is to illustrate how traditional school cultures can be radically changed even in the face of an endless array of challenges and obstacles that are described in Chapter 1. The time for excuses, talk, opinions, and fear needs to end if our goal is really about improving teaching, learning, and leadership outcomes. Leadership is about action, not position or ideas that get pushed around. Leaders need to take action to overcome fixed positions and ideas that simply get put off. This book will lay down the foundation leading to sustainable changes needed in schools that work for kids. We need to continue to push ourselves to create a better school and education system.

When it comes to technology in general, the overall goal is to support learning, not drive instruction. Where digital learning initiatives miss the point is a focus on how technology actually accomplishes this. Schools invest billions of dollars to purchase technology with no real thought as to how it is actually impacting learning. When I routinely ask school leaders how they determine or measure the impact of their technology on student learning, I get blank stares or open declarations that they have no idea. Uncommon learning moves past a bells-and-whistles approach to technology integration to ensure that the tools are having an impact on learning, which is monitored and validated through quality assessments.

The right culture focuses on technology as a tool to enhance learning in a variety of ways. When technology is integrated with purpose, students can create artifacts to demonstrate conceptual mastery, apply an array of acquired skills, illustrate the construction of new knowledge, and be empowered to take ownership over their learning. It also can increase relevance and make the curriculum more contextual. The right culture also provides learning experiences that are aligned to student interests and passions while preparing them to succeed in jobs that have not even been created yet. Uncommon learning initiatives should complement the work that is already taking place in schools while allowing students to clearly see the value in their learning. The key is sustainability and a resulting change that sees innovative learning become an embedded component of school culture as opposed to isolated pockets of excellence. Without the right culture in place for digital learning to be embraced and thrive, there will be only isolated pockets of excellence. Chapter 2 will address the essential elements needed to support an array of uncommon learning initiatives that will be discussed in detail in the subsequent chapters. These elements work in concert with one another to develop school cultures that support uncommon learning across the curriculum, throughout the school, and extending well beyond the school day.

Uncommon Learning Initiatives

The whole premise of uncommon learning is to increase relevance, add context, acquire then apply essential skills, construct new knowledge, and enhance critical literacies. Regardless of what standards you are accountable for, uncommon learning initiatives with and without technology can be integrated seamlessly to foster deeper learning. Chapter 2 will set the stage for the implementation of the following initiatives:

- **Digital learning across the curriculum:** Today's learners yearn to use real-world tools to do real-world work. Effective digital learning environments focus on learning outcomes as opposed to the tools themselves. This chapter will address the basic tenet that the role of technology is to support learning, not drive instruction. The concepts of digital learning will be presented and discussed. Practitioner vignettes providing details on pedagogy, learning activities, and assessment will appear here and throughout subsequent chapters.
- **Makerspaces:** These spaces provide cost-effective ways for any school to transform a dull or underutilized space

into a vibrant learning environment. These spaces compel students to create, tinker, invent, problem solve, collaborate, and think to learn. Makerspaces can be created on any budget and motivate students to learn on their own time. They also become supplemental learning spaces for science, technology, engineering, and mathematics (STEM)-related classes and courses.

- **Blended and virtual learning:** Traditional schooling, as dictated by brick-and-mortar buildings and mainstay pedagogical techniques, no longer meets the diverse learning needs of all students. This chapter will address how schools easily implement both blended and virtual learning opportunities to personalize and individualize instruction with technology. It also will discuss the flipped classroom approach. This new pedagogical technique continues to be implemented across the globe. Pulling from practitioner examples, this chapter will look at many variations of the flipped classroom with an emphasis on how educators themselves can create short, interactive learning experiences that provide more time for the application of concepts during class.

- **Bring your own device (BYOD):** Many students now possess a powerful learning tool in the form of mobile technology. This chapter will address the potential challenges and advantages of implementing a BYOD initiative. Issues such as equity, infrastructure, policy development, digital responsibility, pedagogy, and tools will be discussed. The end result is creating an environment that empowers students to use the tools they possess as mobile learning devices to enhance learning, increase productivity, develop positive digital footprints, and conduct better research.

- **Digital badges and micro-credentials:** Digital badges are beginning to be embraced as a means to acknowledge a particular skill, accomplishment, or quality associated with learning. This chapter will look at how schools have begun to integrate digital badges to acknowledge the informal learning of teachers and formal learning of students.

- **Academies and smaller learning communities:** These programs represent a bold vision and direction based on student interests, national and global need, and intangible skill sets necessary for success. This chapter will examine how schools can create their own unique academy programs on a limited budget to expand course offerings, form mutually beneficial partnerships, and provide authentic learning experiences that students yearn for.
- **Connected learning:** Educators today can learn anytime, from anywhere, with anyone they choose. This paradigm shift eliminates the notion of schools being silos of information and educators feeling that they reside on isolated learning islands. Connected learning shatters the construct of traditional learning options such as conferences and workshops as the only viable means for professional growth. This chapter will provide a foundation for innovative learning using social media that will continuously support uncommon learning.

ORGANIZATION OF THE BOOK

The first two chapters set the stage for why change is needed along with specific strategies and ideas for implementation. After Chapter 2 the flow of the book is such that each subsequent chapter represents a separate uncommon learning initiative. This allows the reader to select a particular focus area of interest without having to read the book cover to cover. Throughout each of these chapters are vignettes illustrating key ideas and implementation tips so that the reader can begin the change process. Relevant links also have been incorporated into these chapters to add depth and provide further details on each initiative. Pertinent graphics and data related to how each initiative has had a positive impact on student achievement also are included throughout the book. An appendix provides additional resources to assist leaders with implementation.

Acknowledgments

The process of writing books becomes much easier when you have ideas and strategies that have been implemented with success and a team working to create a readable manuscript. For Eric, the students at New Milford High School motivated him to work harder to create a school that worked better for them. The resulting transformation not only benefitted his students but also provides a glimpse into what is possible for all schools. Educators such as Laura Fleming, Nicholas Provenzano, Rich Allen, Joanna Westbrook, Scott McLeod, Julie Graber, Tiffany Della Vedova, Daisy Dyer-Duerr, Dierdre DeAngelis, Kanchan Chellani, Alfonso Gonzalez, and Hershey Groff, through their innovative work, provided further support for benefits of uncommon learning techniques. Eric cannot thank these educators or the countless others who are working tirelessly across the globe to implement uncommon learning techniques to create schools that work for kids.

Eric would like to thank the staff of Corwin: Executive Editor Arnis Burvikovs, who has served as his mentor over the past couple of years and provided him with the confidence to take on this project; Associate Editor Andrew Olsen, who's diligent oversight made sure everything was in order;

Ariel Price, who provided invaluable feedback and suggestions on how to improve the manuscript early on; Project Editor Amy Joy Schroller, who moved the process along with precision; and Copy Editor Pam Schroeder, whose attention to detail expedited the production of this book.

PUBLISHER'S ACKNOWLEDGMENTS

Corwin gratefully acknowledges the contributions of the following reviewers:

Kristina Moody
Intervention Strategist
Bay High School
Bay Saint Louis, MS

Tanna Nicely
Principal
Knox County Schools
Knoxville, TN

Pamela Murphy
High School English Teacher
Trevor Day School
New York, NY

Paul Solarz
Teacher and Author of *Learn
   Like a PIRATE*
Westgate Elementary School
Arlington Heights, IL

About the Author

Eric C. Sheninger is a Senior Fellow and Thought Leader on Digital Leadership with the International Center for Leadership in Education (ICLE). Prior to this he was the award-winning Principal at New Milford High School. Under his leadership his school became a globally recognized model for innovative practices. Eric oversaw the successful implementation of several sustainable change initiatives that radically transformed the learning culture at his school while increasing achievement.

His work focuses on leading and learning in the digital age as a model for moving schools and districts forward. This has led to the formation of the Pillars of Digital Leadership, a framework for all educators to initiate sustainable change to transform school cultures. As a result Eric has emerged as an innovative leader, best-selling author, and sought-after speaker. His main focus is purposeful integration of technology to facilitate student learning, improve communications with stakeholders, enhance public relations, create a positive brand presence, discover opportunity, transform learning spaces, and help educators grow professionally.

Eric is a Center for Digital Education Top 30 Award recipient (2014), Bammy Award winner (2013), NASSP Digital Principal Award winner (2012), PDK Emerging Leader Award recipient (2012), winner of Learning Forward's Excellence in Professional Practice Award (2012), Google Certified Innovator, Adobe Education Leader, and ASCD 2011 Conference Scholar. He is also the author of the best-selling book *Digital Leadership: Changing Paradigms for Changing Times* (Corwin, 2014).

He also has contributed on education for the *Huffington Post* and was named to the NSBA "20 to Watch" list in 2010 for technology leadership. *TIME Magazine* also identified Eric as having one of the 140 Best Twitter Feeds in 2014. He now presents and speaks nationally to assist other school leaders to embrace and effectively utilize technology. His blog, "A Principal's Reflections," was selected as Best School Administrator Blog in 2013 and 2011 by Edublogs.

Eric began his career in education as a Science Teacher at Watchung Hills Regional High School, where he taught a variety of subjects (biology, chemistry, marine biology, and ecology) and coached several sports (ice hockey, football, and lacrosse). He then transitioned into the field of educational administration as an Athletic Director, Supervisor of Physical Education and Health, and Vice Principal in the New Milford School District. During his administrative career he has served as District Affirmative Action Officer and was the president of the New Milford Administrator's Association. During his tenure as a high school principal, he successfully implemented numerous initiatives including a new teacher evaluation system (McREL), oversaw Common Core implementation, and initiated a new grading philosophy. Eric received his MEd in educational administration from East Stroudsburg University, BS in biology from Salisbury University, and his BS in marine and environmental science from the University of Maryland Eastern Shore. To learn more about Eric's work, visit ericsheninger.com, or follow @E_Sheninger on Twitter. Watch his TEDx Talk on creating schools that work for kids at http://tinyurl.com/Schools4Kids.

The Challenges
That Schools and
Educators Face

As society continues to rapidly change due to the evolution of a global economy and advances in technology, schools continue to function in the same way as they did 100 years ago. Students, teachers, and leaders are changing as a result of the proliferation of technology in the real world. Our information society needs people who can effectively manage and use ever-increasing amounts of information to solve complex problems and to make decisions in the face of uncertainty (An & Reigeluth, 2011). This presents a bit of a paradox as schools as the traditional factory model of education is incompatible with the evolving demands of the information age (Reigeluth, 1996). Despite decades of national, state, and local promotion of educational uses of technology, classroom practice in most schools has changed little from that of the mid-20th century (Means, 2010). This challenge is compounded by issues related to aging infrastructure, inequity in funding, and a global focus on standardization.

INFRASTRUCTURE AND MONEY

New Milford High School was built in 1928. Architecture back then was profoundly beautiful as buildings were designed to resemble other structures of that time period. Not only were these buildings aesthetically pleasing, but they were also built with high-quality materials throughout, including hardwoods and brick. When looking at aged school buildings like this one, everything on the outside looks fine, but the inside is another story. One must remember that the internal structure of the majority of school complexes in the world was built during a time when there was literally no technology. This poses a huge obstacle for educators and students wanting to access the many treasures of the Internet that ubiquitous access to Wi-Fi provides.

Not only are schools with aging infrastructures having challenges meeting the needs of digital learners and educators who want to effectively integrate technology but rural schools as well, who lack access. The emergence of technology as a critical component of education has presented rural districts with an invaluable tool for overcoming the problems created by sparse and remote populations. But the same districts often face barriers to effective implementation of technology from lack of infrastructure and funding to a shortage of tech-savvy teachers, staff, and potential community partners (Gordon, 2011).

The physical conditions in many schools provide educators with steep obstacles to overcome when providing a world-class learning experience to students. This is where financial stresses begin to take their toll. The recent recession resulted in the loss of funding for schools all over the world. As teachers were cut, precious funds that remained were used to retain staff and procure essential items that were required to assist with teaching and learning on a daily basis. Many schools then experienced drastic cuts to much-needed professional development opportunities while neglected buildings continued to become worse and worse. Without a clear plan to allocate funds to infrastructure that will support innovative instructional practices, the pressure to stay the course and continue doing what has been done for many years persists. The result of this challenge has been a widening poverty gap in the United States that thwarts many essential change initiatives from taking place. Without the proper funds a lack of access to technology and the Internet inhibits learners from using powerful tools and techniques that can unleash creativity while focusing on essential skill sets that the global job market demands.

In light of these challenges national initiatives have taken root that focus on ubiquitous connectivity for all students. More funding also is becoming available for school construction projects the address aging infrastructure issues. Creative educators are finding ways to bridge the gap when funding comes up short by forming mutually beneficial partnerships with educational technology companies. All of this is made possible through the use of free social media tools to connect, engage, and form relationships to move learning forward. Chapter 9 will provide a road map for educators looking to take advantage of connecting with social media to spur uncommon learning pathways in their schools.

CONTROL AND COMPLIANCE

For more than a century, the industrial model of education did a fantastic job of preparing students for careers. Those careers are no longer relevant in today's rapidly changing world. With obvious remnants of this system still in place, new changes are being pushed through under the guise of education reform. Instead of preparing students for an industrialized world, the education system is now being tasked with preparing all learners to be college and career ready to compete globally with their peers. However, there still has been little change in the overall structure and function of many schools. In essence students are being prepared for a world that no longer exists, even though the objective has changed.

The education system is not changing fast enough to account for societal shifts. There also tends to be a focus on control and compliance to maintain models of teaching and learning that have long outlived their usefulness. Many leaders have assimilated into a culture of compliancy and taken a more subversive role implementing mandates (Ball, 2000). When schools focus primarily on compliance, they tend to concentrate school improvement efforts on what and how they can be measured (Bernhardt, 2013). The failed legacy of No Child Left Behind (NCLB) should provide a stark reminder that increasing the amount of weight standardized tests have on measuring school performance will not achieve the desired outcome. Diane Ravitch (2013) brings some additional light to current education reform. She explains that the unnatural focus on testing has produced perverse but predictable results. It has narrowed curriculums to testable subjects to the exclusion of the arts and the full capaciousness of culture. She goes on to explain how it has encouraged the manipulation of scores on state exams. "Teaching to the test, once considered unprofessional and unethical," is now "common" (Ravitch, 2013).

So again our education system is in a pickle consisting of an outdated model and the pressure to prepare students for an absurd amount of testing days throughout the school year. The world does not rest on standardized tests. Success now lies in one's ability to create solutions to problems, collaborate with peers to meet a goal, communicate effectively, and develop unique ideas that can change things for the better.

Unfortunately autonomy has been slowly stripped away from many educators and schools, something that has defined our country for decades. Even with an outdated model, we still have found ways to provide innovative pathways to unleash a passion for learning among our students. Control has been a challenge that some have chosen to overcome. In the face of adversity, educators have strived to overcome it to benefit our most precious resource—students. However, the current rhetoric and testing blitz that is upon us seeks not only to undermine what makes education special but to control us to a point that will break the morale of many, if it hasn't already.

There is another type of control that we need to acknowledge that is prevalent in virtually every school in the world. This is the control fostered by administration and teachers as to how learning should, and will, be structured. This hits home for me on many fronts, as I was guilty of this years ago. We are often our own worst enemies as we work hard to control what students can do in school or classrooms. This stems from the fact that we don't want to give up control. Compliancy has worked for so long, and quite frankly we don't trust students or even our own teachers. What we don't know and understand, we fear. So we react by trying to control every facet of school structure, function, and learning.

I was just like every other principal. My narrow focus was on sustaining a school culture focused on rules, compliance, conformity, and preserving the status quo. The end goal was to make sure that standardized test scores increased (or at least didn't go down) and traditions were preserved. On the inside everything was great. Students and staff seemed happy, while the community was supportive of our efforts. Each monotonous day began with students arriving to school and then going directly to their first-period classes, where they sat in desks arranged in orderly rows. After listening to the daily announcements, the delivery of instruction began. My compliant students then went through their rigid eight-period day schedule with each class lasting 48 minutes. At the end of each class, an annoying bell would notify everyone in the school that it was time to continue through the repetitive process. Throw in a few specialized programs, assemblies, and pep rallies, and this was basically the schedule we all followed each and every day.

It is scary to think that the culture I describe here is still prevalent in the majority of schools across the country. The reality is that school for most students is the polar opposite of the real world. Thus they come to school knowing that they will sit through endless lectures, endure the same lessons that have been delivered year after year, be assigned homework that does nothing to support learning, be given assessments that require little thought because they are easy to grade, and have to succumb to numerous rules that are meant to make sure they conform more than learn. Getting through the curriculum aligned to Common Core has become the driving force in many schools as pressure is mounting with high-stakes testing looming right around the corner. This was me for many years.

YOU NEED TO WANT TO CHANGE

Change is a word that is thrown around in education circles more and more each day. The fact of the matter is that education has to change dramatically, but how this is initiated should no longer be a contentious topic for discussion or debate. It is relatively agreed upon that the structure and function of the majority of schools across the globe no longer meet the needs of students in the digital age. There is a quiet revolution that is gaining steam as more and more educators and students push back against the very policies and mandates that have been forced upon them. You need to decide if it is worth it to conform or to carve out your own path instead to provide your students with the education and learning experiences they deserve.

Meaningful change has and always will begin at the individual level. This is also where it is sustained to the point that it becomes an embedded component of school or district culture. It does not rely on someone being in a leadership position in a traditional sense but more so on a desire to want to change professional practice. This is the point where all educators and students must realize that they have the capacity to lead change. School leaders need to remove barriers to the change process, remove the fear of failure, provide autonomy, and empower teachers to drive change at the classroom level.

These successes can then be promoted within the school and district to serve as a catalyst for cultural transformation. The same holds true for both teachers and administrators when it comes to students, who happen to be our number one stakeholder group. Schools should be designed to meet the needs of our students, but if they are not given a seat at the table and allowed to be a focal point of change efforts that ultimately impact them, a golden opportunity is missed. Never underestimate the power that you have to make your school, district, and the entire education system better. Be the change that you wish to see in education, and others will follow. After all, real change comes from colleagues modeling expectations to others, not from those with titles.

EXCUSES HOLD US BACK

When was the last time you came up with an excuse to get out of doing something that you did not want to do? Chances are it was today or sometime in the not-so-distant past. We even use them when there is actually no hope of getting out of the activity for which the excuse was derived.

As I was doing some research recently for a presentation, I came across a fantastic slide that really put into perspective the concept of excuses. "If something is important to us, we will find a way. If not, then we'll make an excuse." On a professional level excuses can, and often do, have dramatic negative impacts when it comes to change on many levels. If education is good for one thing, it is for making excuses not to move forward. Schools continue to move along as they did more than 100 years ago. The feeling is that our system of education has worked so well during this time; why change now? In this example the common excuse that many educators use not to change is that student achievement, defined by standardized test scores, has remained high; so if it isn't broke, why fix it? When it comes to technology, excuses are as abundant as traffic in New York City during rush hour. Regardless of the scenario, here are the most common excuses that I have either used myself or experienced during my years as a practitioner:

- I don't have time.
- This will cost too much money.
- It is just another thing that I have to do.
- It has worked well for so long, so why change now?
- Student safety and security will be compromised.
- Students will cheat and be off task, so I am not allowing them to use devices.
- We can't implement this due to the Common Core and an array of state mandates.

Excuses are fueled by elements such as fear of change, a desire to protect the status quo, lack of education or knowledge, top-down leadership, micromanagement, and the unwillingness to take risks. By no means is this list comprehensive, but it does provide a fairly solid foundation for why excuses dominate the education profession. Sustainable changes leading to cultural transformation in schools can and will happen only when one moves from a fixed to a growth mind-set. It is imperative in our respective positions that we create a shared vision that focuses on solutions to problems as opposed to taking the path of least resistance exemplified by the excuse.

The best way to accomplish this is to help others see the value in new initiatives and ways of thinking. Provide a clear rationale for change tied to research and examples from other schools where these initiatives have been successfully implemented. Ensure that support structures are in place such as professional development, autonomy, availability of resources, and the establishment of a feedback loop. This will set the stage for empowering others to embrace the change while discovering the value of it all themselves. Most importantly model the expectations that you wish to see implemented, and take action.

SUMMARY

The whole premise behind this book is it to provide relevancy, meaning, and authenticity in the teaching and learning process. It hinges upon our ability to provide an environment and activities that unleash our students' passion for learning and allows them to create artifacts of learning with the tools of their choice to demonstrate conceptual mastery. Additionally, it relies on a bold vision to grant students and educators the autonomy to take risks, learn from failure, and then adapt as needed. Meaningful change will happen only if we begin to give up control and establish a culture built on trust and respect. If we truly want to prepare the next generation of thinkers, doers, inventors, and change agents, we must give up control, trust students and educators, and work to develop a better system that will produce desired outcomes. Educators must acknowledge the real challenges that they are faced with each day but work to develop solutions to overcome them. Challenges should not be seen as insurmountable obstacles to change but rather opportunities to do things differently and better. The end result will be the proliferation of uncommon learning strategies that in time will become common.

Culture Shock

Schools should be . . . inviting to all students. There should be a feeling of respect, trust, and partnership between students, parents, and teachers. In such an environment, students will be given the opportunity to express themselves, and their self-determination will rise, knowing that they can make a difference.

—Kathleen Cushman (1994)

Schools need to overcome an array of challenges if we are to create meaningful, relevant, and applicable learning experiences and environments for our students. These challenges work to influence the structure and function of school districts, buildings, and classrooms negatively. At New Milford High School (NMHS) we had to overcome an array of challenges discussed in the previous chapter including infrastructure, lack of money, no technology, a challenging and diverse population, federal and state reforms, a resistant staff, time, and parents who wanted their children taught the same way they were.

Reforms that strive for educational excellence will fail unless they are meaningfully linked to schools' unique cultures (Deal & Peterson, 1999). To begin the change process leading to a transformation of school learning culture, we must identify elements that are pivotal to success. This chapter will focus on specific and identifiable elements that impact a school's learning culture based on practitioner experiences. Each is an essential part of a shared vision and resulting plan of action to transform the culture into one where uncommon learning practices are not isolated examples of excellence but rather systemic initiatives that have become embedded within and across the entire system.

THE ELEMENTS OF A SCHOOL LEARNING CULTURE

Student learning is impacted by a variety of elements prevalent inside and outside the school environment. Students are the key component of any school learning culture. All policies and initiatives are inherently geared to provide each and every child with the proper academic and social foundation to excel in college or careers. For students in the digital age, the challenge has become even more difficult as schools are now tasked with preparing learners for jobs that do not even exist yet while struggling to engage them for six to eight hours out of the school day. Students yearn for an educational experience that caters to their interests, innate desire for expressive creativity, and a need for play. Cultures that do not provide these experiences fail to resonate with a finicky learner who finds more value and meaning though self-directed learning opportunities outside of school.

Possibly the most important factor impacting student learning is the teachers who comprise a particular school. Studies have shown that there is no bigger influence on student achievement then that of a quality teacher (Hattie, 2012). The individuals who inhabit these positions have the potential to impact the life of a child positively each and every day. It is no secret then that teachers play crucial roles in a school's learning culture, but they also can be the predominant factor in creating an environment toward which students feel no connection or relevancy.

Great teachers inspire students to follow their passions through authentic work that integrates a variety of disciplines. They push students to develop essential understandings through the creation of learning artifacts to demonstrate conceptual mastery. Most importantly they create safe, inclusive classrooms that address diverse learning styles through the differentiation of the instructional process. The end result is a greater appreciation for learning and the development of essential skill sets that put students in a better position to succeed not only in school but also in life.

The climate of a school provides a foundation for the learning culture. This is influenced not only by the teachers on staff but also the administration and support personnel working collaboratively to create a learning experience that is valued by students. In addition to curriculum, courses, and a schedule, the climate of a school is molded by numerous factors such as the budget, evaluation of instruction, professional learning, extracurricular programs, support services, facilities, code of conduct, and other pertinent policies. School climate also is heavily influenced by initiatives that are implemented to make the school experience more reflective of the real world that students are immersed in outside the instructional day.

THE ESSENTIAL INGREDIENTS

When one begins to think about the change process, the foundational step always seems to be the role of a leader. I was always under the impression that it was the leader who was the actual change agent, but my experiences helping schools implement an array of initiatives to improve school culture have taught me otherwise. A leader's main role is to create an environment that fosters change. After all you rarely see, if at all, assistant principals, principals, or superintendents in a position to transform teaching and learning when they are not directly working with students every day. Therefore true leaders remove obstacles and challenges to clear a path for those individuals who actually do have the capacity. They do so through a combination of essential ingredients that not only lay the foundation but also ensure that it withstands the test of time. More than 30 years of research have shown that these elements have all been found to contribute to the effect of leadership to change school culture and positively impact student achievement (Waters, Marzano, & McNulty, 2003).

VISION AND COMMUNICATION

Effective leaders help their schools develop or endorse visions that embody the best thinking about teaching and learning while inspiring others to reach for ambitions goals (Leithwood & Riehl, 2003). Change can begin only when everyone is on the same page or at the very least has an idea of the rationale behind decisions that will move a school in a different direction. This requires the formation of a shared vision in which all stakeholder groups are not only represented but also have direct input in the processes to be implemented. Leading with vision is critical to the success of schools (Wallace, Engel, & Mooney, 1997). A shared vision relies on shared leadership. Hughes and Pickeral (2013) outline five shared leadership strategies that will help build a coherent vision that is embraced by all:

1. Set clear parameters to create balanced power and establish leadership as a partnership.

2. Engage all stakeholders in working together toward a shared purpose.

3. Ensure all participants share responsibility and accountability.

4. Recognize and embrace diverse perspectives in the group.

5. Teach and value inner strength in all participants in shared leadership.

Teachers have extraordinary leadership capabilities, and their leadership is a major untapped resource for our nation's schools (Barth, 1990). We must remember this when developing a shared vision. In addition to the normal cast of characters that typically comprises stakeholder groups, it is time to consistently include students in this process. After all, the premise behind any change should always be about creating a school culture that focuses on the academic success as well as the social and emotional well-being of students. Teachers can employ the same shared leadership elements in their classrooms with students to create a shared vision for learning and achievement.

To avoid common challenges and obstacles previously addressed, it is imperative that initial conversations specifically address the following:

1. What are we going to change?

2. Why is the change needed?

3. How are we going to initiate and sustain this change?

4. How will we ensure the effectiveness of the change effort?

A clear, well-articulated vision sets the stage for the time and effort that will be put into following through on a sometimes long, arduous journey. Listening to the ideas of supporters as well as the naysayers and antagonists provides needed support down the line when and if things do not go as planned. As I gained more experience as a principal, I learned to listen more intently to both sides of a debate, allowed anyone to offer ideas that could improve our existing culture, and most importantly tried to include some of that feedback into the overall implementation plan. This advice extends well beyond that of the administrator and teacher relationship during the change process. It is just as important for teachers to enact a similar process with students when looking to change classroom policies and learning practices.

Once meetings with stakeholders have commenced and there is some sort of consensus on a plan moving forward, communication becomes pivotal. Regardless of how well a plan of action is agreed upon and developed by a core group of stakeholders, poor communication can undermine the effort before it even has a chance to take off. Skillful leaders focus attention on key aspects of the school's vision and communicate the vision clearly and convincingly while inviting interchange with multiple stakeholders through participatory communication activities (Leithwood & Riehl, 2003). Clear communication strategies address the essential questions listed earlier in this chapter and work to ease rising anxiety levels that are always associated with any change process. People don't want to be told that change is needed or be in a position where they feel blindsided by a new course without any rhyme or reason. Effective communication tactics lay out all the pertinent details that address the what, why, and where while mitigating the small group of underminers present in any organization, school, or classroom. If the communication fails, so will the change initiative.

In today's digital world educators and leaders should take advantage of a variety of pathways to meet stakeholders where they are to communicate more effectively. When we began to move numerous change initiatives forward at NMHS, I used a multifaceted approach that combined traditional techniques with new-age media. So in addition to memos, meetings (teacher and parents), newsletters, and e-mail, I also was able to amplify the same message more profoundly using social media tools such as Twitter, Facebook, and Instagram. I also leveraged other tools to communicate the change initiatives through the use of our school mobile app and QR codes. The end result was a consistent, uniform message broadcast in a variety of ways that was available to more stakeholders than ever before.

FLEXIBLE PLANNING AND LEARNING PATHWAYS

A sound, well-thought-out plan that is meticulously implemented is usually the hallmark characteristic of any change initiative. In addition to the what, why, and how, consistent monitoring of the plan as well as an assessment of the outcomes are key. Regardless of the level of planning on either an innovative learning activity or school-wide initiative, the chances are something might go wrong. It is important to realize that even with all the planning in the world, unforeseeable situations arise. Understanding this prior to any type of change initiative, large or small, will prepare you if an obstacle arises. Don't let these little detours distract you from the bigger picture at hand, which is creating a more relevant learning culture for your students.

Flexibility becomes even more important when integrating technology. Technology not only has the ability to enhance learning while allowing students to create meaningful artifacts that demonstrate conceptual mastery, but also it is known to fail once in a while. In some schools it fails more often than not. Teachers in particular have to be cognizant of this fact and prepared for inconsistent Wi-Fi connections, slow speeds, blocked Web sites, antiquated tools, and unexplained reboots. This is particularly important when being observed by an administrator as this high-pressure situation has been known to throw many teachers into a vortex of uncontrolled anxiety.

Uncommon learning only thrives in school cultures that see flexibility as an asset. Teachers will not only need to foresee certain potential issues with technology, but they also will need to plan for new types of learning experiences that extend learning time both in and out of school. This then requires a school culture that promotes and supports learning activities that might take more than the required class period. For example, many of my teachers began to use videoconference technology such as Skype and Google Hangouts to bring guest speakers into their classrooms to provide a greater sense of relevance for their students. Not only did they have to account for the unique schedules of the speakers, but also they had to deal with time zone challenges. As we gave up control, more flexibility was imparted on teachers to either extend the class period or pull students from other classes to hold a videoconference.

Rigid school schedules and archaic policies should not dictate the types of learning experiences students can and should have available to them today. Staying the course without adapting to bumps in the road will inherently result in failure. Flexibility avoids common pitfalls that plague all types of change initiatives where control dominates the school culture. Policies and normal procedures should act only to guide school function, not create a sterilized atmosphere where learning is anything but fun, relevant, or meaningful. It is more than OK to take a detour now and then to ensure that change is implemented strategically and with purpose. This will become a reality only if flexibility is an embedded component of the school culture.

Flexibility also should be applied to classroom instruction. All too often learning becomes a one-size-fits-all approach where students are tasked with demonstrating what they know the same way. This is extremely prevalent in project-based learning activities where students have to create a presentation that will eventually be assessed. In many cases the standard has become directing all students to develop PowerPoint presentations, which ultimately results in role reversal where students are imparting direct instruction upon their peers. Uncommon learning materializes when students are given flexibility as to how they can demonstrate what they know and have learned. In this case teachers give students a choice as to the tools and resulting products they want to use and create that are aligned to the same standards and learning outcomes associated with PowerPoint presentations. The difference is a much more authentic, rich product that does a better job of quantifying meaningful learning and skill acquisition.

AUTONOMY AND OWNERSHIP

The most successful students are those who feel real "ownership" of their education. In all the best performing school systems . . . "students feel they personally can make a difference in their own outcomes and that education will make a difference for their future."

— Quote from Thomas Freidman (2013),
who is quoting Andreas Schleicher

Whose learning is it anyway? This question is not posed enough in schools. The reality is that schooling and education are more in line with what adults want in the classroom, school, and district as opposed to what's best for students. The fact is that students should own their learning and play a major role in the development of activities that are meant for them to showcase the construction of new knowledge and essential skill acquisition. Autonomy, in the context of education, is the ability to take charge of one's learning (Holec, 1981). The term *autonomy* has been adapted over the years and is now used in a variety of ways (Benson & Voller, 1997, p. 2):

- for situations in which learners study entirely on their own
- for a set of skills that can be learned and applied in self-directed learning
- for an inborn capacity that is suppressed by institutional education
- for the exercise of learners' responsibility for their own learning
- for the right of learners to determine the direction of their own learning

When students have a certain level of autonomy as to what, why, how, and where they learn, it leads to a more vested interest in the experience. They have a greater sense of responsibility and self-motivation to engage in lessons or learning activities regardless of complexity, time, or content area. This process leads to ownership of learning on the part of the student where he or she is placed in a position to experience the value and meaning of the experience. The importance of autonomy cannot be overstated. Jang and Reeve (2005) found that an increase in learner autonomy resulted in the following:

- greater engagement
- more positive emotionality
- greater conceptual learning
- preference for optimal challenge
- greater school retention (vs. dropping out)
- higher academic achievement

Uncommon learning starts and ends with the student. Inquiry can be used as a powerful catalyst with or without the effective integration of technology. When students are placed front and center in the learning process, the stage is set for a

Figure 2.1		Inquiry Framework: Levels of Student Ownership			

inquiry mode	research question	study system and methods	data collection	analysis and presentation	scholarly goal of the activity
closed-ended demonstration	given	given	given	given	teach existing knowledge by showing or guiding students to it
guided inquiry	given	given	student/ given	student	
bounded inquiry	student/ given	student/given	student	student	teach the process of knowledge construction
open-ended inquiry	student/ given	student	student	student	
collaboration w/researcher	given	student/given	student/ given	student/given	create knowledge new to discipline

Source: From "Technology and Inquiry Based Learning." Webpage originally created by Dr. Joyce L. Morris. Revised (with permission of the author) on March 4, 2011, by Sandra A. Lathem, EdD, The University of Vermont. Accessed August 5, 2015 from http://www.uvm.edu/~slathem/inquiry/inquiry21st.htm.

greater focus on critical thinking and problem-solving skills. Technology can be seamlessly integrated to increase student autonomy, resulting in ownership of learning. The framework from Sundberg and Moncada (1994), Ohlhorst (1995), D'Avanzo (1996), and Grant and Vatnick (1998) takes this idea of ownership and applies it to inquiry-based learning. The result is a kind of spectrum analyzing the nature of teaching inquiry, moving closed-ended demonstration to open-ended inquiry and even collaboration with the researchers themselves (Heick, 2013).

At the top of the chart, most of the components of inquiry learning—the questions, research system, data collection methods, and forms of presentation and publishing—are all given by the teacher to the student. As students increasingly take on ownership in pursuit of more open-ended inquiry, less is given by the teacher, and is instead "owned" and provided by the students (Heick, 2013). With inquiry at the heart of student-centered learning, technology becomes a seamless fit for students to then demonstrate what they have learned through the creation of an artifact.

Autonomy and ownership can create unprecedented learning opportunities for students if teachers and administrators are willing to give up control and allow learners to explore their passions and interests while helping to develop a growth mind-set in students. Students with growth mind-sets have been found to be more motivated to learn and exert effort and outperform those with fixed mind-sets (Blackwell, Trzesniewski, & Dweck, 2007). Bold educators have begun to integrate these elements in classrooms through a concept called Genius Hour. Genius Hour provides students freedom to design their own learning during a set period of time during school. It allows students to explore their own curiosity through a self-manifested sense of purpose and study while within the support system of the classroom (Heick, 2014). Genius Hour is most notably associated with Google, where employees were able to spend up to 20 percent of their time working on projects they were interested in or passionate

Figure 2.2

Six Principles of Genius Hour in the Classroom

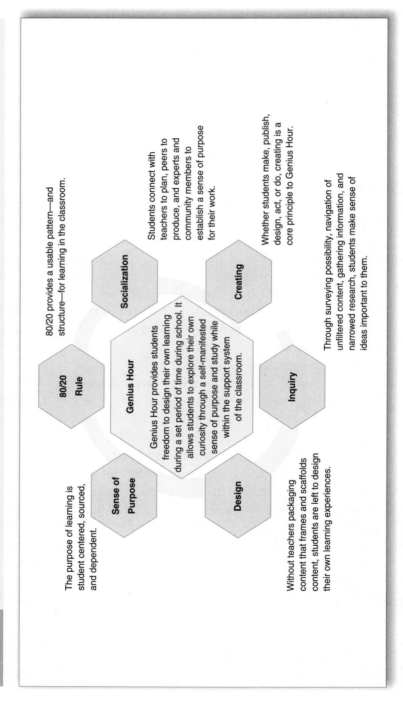

The purpose of learning is student centered, sourced, and dependent.

Sense of Purpose

80/20 provides a usable pattern—and structure—for learning in the classroom.

80/20 Rule

Students connect with teachers to plan, peers to produce, and experts and community members to establish a sense of purpose for their work.

Socialization

Genius Hour

Genius Hour provides students freedom to design their own learning during a set period of time during school. It allows students to explore their own curiosity through a self-manifested sense of purpose and study while within the support system of the classroom.

Whether students make, publish, design, act, or do, creating is a core principle to Genius Hour.

Creating

Without teachers packaging content that frames and scaffolds content, students are left to design their own learning experiences.

Design

Through surveying possibility, navigation of unfiltered content, gathering information, and narrowed research, students make sense of ideas important to them.

Inquiry

about. The study and work was motivated intrinsically, not extrinsically. The big idea for Google was that employees motivated by curiosity and passion would be happier, more creative, and more productive, which benefitted the company in terms of morale, "off-Genius" productivity, and "on-Genius" performance (Heick, 2014).

COLLABORATION

Can't we all just get along? The concept of a sandbox is that it is in inclusive space where groups of children congregate around one simple goal—play. School is akin to a giant sandbox where adults possessing dramatically different personalities congregate on a professional level with one lofty goal—educating students. As kids, our parents encouraged us to play nice with others in the sandbox, and this should be no different in a school environment. The field of education has been moving from a profession that hoarded ideas, lessons, and successful strategies to one that is openly willing to share this bounty with as many passionate educators as possible. Innovation and change is a collective process, and schools that get this concept have personnel who routinely collaborate among each other and with those outside of their schools. "Together we are better" is the motto that change agents abide by.

Regardless of whether or not teachers are collaborating with their colleagues either face-to-face or virtually, the results benefit students. Empowering teachers to work and collaborate toward a common goal makes them aware of their responsibilities and the important role each one of them plays in the work (Hughes & Pickeral, 2013). For example, how can an English teacher help to develop critical literacy across the curriculum? What follows is a story of how NMHS teachers have collaborated with English teacher Joanna Westbrook to create authentic literacy tasks in each of their disciplines. You see how a science teacher, a social studies teacher, and an art teacher provided their own unique takes on how Common Core and 21st-century learning goals affected what went on in the classroom.

The first story comes from the work of biology teacher Lynn Torpie. Science teachers for the 21st century are tasked with producing citizens who are conversant with the language of science and who can read, make sense of, and make decisions about scientific issues. Optimally, they inspire students to pursue a career in which they will be posing relevant questions and using research and inquiry to answer those questions to contribute to humanity's general body of knowledge or, through technology and engineering, solve problems. Literacy skills are the foundation upon which these outcomes are built.

But many science teachers can be daunted by the mandate to incorporate English language skills into the curriculum. They have neither the training to assess such skills nor the language to develop such assessments. As a result science teachers are concerned about their students' weak explanatory writing skills and would like to see those skills improve. But they desperately need help. While each can develop assessments that approximate authentic science writing tasks, they need help identifying the literacy elements they should be assessing. Lynn in particular needed guidance in phrasing a rubric so that it was clear to both students and teachers what she was looking for when assessing literacy in science. Even more importantly, she needed to partner and collaborate with English teachers to provide the scaffolding necessary for her students to write informational text with increasing clarity.

This led to a conversation about the use of infographics to assess critical literacy skills. Lynn began the year with a conversation with ninth-grade English language arts (ELA) teacher Joanna Westbrook about how the cognitive learning goals in science class connect to the cognitive learning goals in English class. What grew out of that conversation was an infographic project (Appendix A). For this project, Lynn had her students collect data then present them graphically using infographics such as a bar graph, column graph, pie chart, or hierarchy. In addition, she required students to explain how the data compared to other representative data, draw conclusions, and make specific recommendations based on the data they presented. In the end students engaged in a much more relevant learning activity where the following Common Core Standards were addressed: WHST.9-10.6; WHST.9-10.8; and WHST.9-10.9.

Learning about history offers meaningful and authentic opportunities for students to express their knowledge of the subject matter through writing and discourse. History teachers can benefit from working collaboratively with an English teacher by working together to develop activities that engage students in analyzing and synthesizing content—then applying those skills to authentic writing opportunities. Thus a collaboration between ELA teacher Joanna Westbrook and history teacher Colleen Tambuscio began.

One semester Colleen was presented with a group of students actively engaged in the content and who had expressed, through their development of quality work products, a deeper interest in the subject matter. She decided to approach Joanna with an advanced text on the subject of Nazi ideology for students in an elective course on the Holocaust and genocide. The text included the principles of Nazi ideology that she had taught to students in two classroom lessons. Her goal was to engage the students in the chapters that dealt with non-Jewish victims to broaden their historical framework on the subject matter and to allow students to understand the many layers that encompassed Nazi ideology.

The result was curating an exhibit in history. To accomplish this goal, Joanna helped Colleen develop a "Become a Curator" task with the idea that groups of students would create an exhibit focused on one particular victim group from the Holocaust. Here are example groups:

- Enemies of the Regime: political opponents, Jehovah's Witnesses, and homosexuals
- Territorial Threats: Polish and Soviet civilians and Polish prisoners of war
- Racial Enemies: Germans with mental and physical disabilities, African Germans, and the Roma-Sinti

Because students often experience history through museum learning, either within the walls of a museum or through online exhibitions, this provided an authentic method of engaging students in learning. To begin, Colleen asked students to utilize a specific chapter in Nazi ideology and the Holocaust by the U.S. Holocaust Memorial Museum to research their assigned cluster of non-Jewish victims of Nazi oppression. A description of the project can be found in Appendix A. Common Core standards addressed included the following: RH.9-10.3; WHST.9-10.2; WHST.9-10.4; WHST.9-10.5; and WHST.9-10.8.

For effective Common Core implementation, the same skills must be taught, reinforced, and assessed across the curriculum. This becomes a reality only through collaboration. Art teacher Lisette Morel firmly believed that writing and literacy skills in the arts are crucial if educators want to empower students with the 21st-century skills needed to engage and question the world they live in rather than merely occupy a seat on the sidelines in life. As a working artist, she recognizes how writing is utilized to convey and make connections for her audience. And like all artists, Lisette uses her artist statements to clarify and to provide insight into her work. These statements provide the viewer an inside glimpse into the artistic process and the artist's thinking.

In the art classroom reading, writing, and art making should be happening simultaneously. It was important for Lisette's students to acquire background information on artists and to learn the art-making process. But it was even more important that they gained expertise in describing, evaluating, and engaging in critical discourse about art. She was not concerned with the regurgitation of art history dates and names and meaningless artist information onto paper. No one needs another report on an artist. What she was more interested in was that her students learned during the creating process. It was important for Lisette's students to understand why artists choose certain themes, why they choose certain art processes, why imagery and ideas change, and what connections to world history are apparent. But like her science and social studies colleagues mentioned previously, she too needed guidance to develop literacy components that encouraged her students to build on their visual imagery and insight.

As a result Lisette collaborated with Joanna to create writing components that supported what students were learning in art. One such assignment was the creation of artist statements to accompany their finished pieces for exhibition. They used exemplar texts from a field trip to the Metropolitan Museum of Modern Art in New York City as students worked to create statements that mirrored the professional standards of the art world. This assignment gave them experience in articulating their processes and in writing clear statements that described their own intended effects. They then created a rubric that balanced the literacy demands of the Common Core with the content Lisette wanted to see in their finished pieces. A full description of the assignment can be viewed in Appendix A. The following Common Core Standards were addressed: WHST.9-10.2; WHST.9-10.4; and WHST.9-10.9.

English teachers are the lynchpin for the Common Core and other higher standards in our buildings—the new standards combine the critical literacy and thinking skills that have been addressed during instruction for years and challenge them to find new ways for our kids to interact with and learn content. English teachers know that writing in the content area can no longer be centered on tired, recycled five-paragraph essays students write year after year—the idea of making the content classes into extensions of the English class just does not have traction.

In Joanna's mind English teachers have to work harder for their colleagues and for students than merely suggesting the same old essay about a scientist for science class, the repetitive research report about a hero for social studies, or the Van Gogh PowerPoint for art class. What they bring to the table when they collaborate with their content colleagues has to be rich and has to push kids to interact with text and present their ideas using the authentic discourse of each discipline. This work is hard and requires ELA teachers to listen to their colleagues as they describe the types of reading and writing that will move kids forward within their discipline. In the three tasks described, you see real content coupled with real literacy in ways that apportion reading and writing throughout the curriculum and that broaden students' literacy preparation. This would never have become a reality without collaboration.

Modeling

I remember the early years when I became a connected educator and was using social media to take my professional learning to unprecedented levels. Each day I was acquiring new resources and ideas from other educators who were openly sharing them on Twitter. In particular I was intrigued by how some educators were using Skype to facilitate virtual field trips and bring in guest speakers. This got me excited, so I shared the idea with my staff in the most effective way possible at the time. The result was the crafting of a memo, verbal reinforcement at faculty meetings, and constant reminders through daily e-mail blasts. I even kid around today that my leadership style was death by memo. In my mind I did everything right to articulate the rationale for integrating this new technology to support learning. However, I became baffled as months went by and not one staff member had even attempted to use Skype in his or her classroom.

This experience was an early reminder of the importance of modeling. At first I was upset that my enthusiasm for how technology could improve learning experiences for my students wasn't embraced. Instead of sulking I figured that maybe the missing element was the fact that I myself had never even downloaded Skype, let alone used it. This motivated me to reach out to one of my teachers, and together we learned how to use Skype. Within five minutes we downloaded the application and began to use it from different areas of the school. At the next faculty meeting I modeled for my staff how simple it was to videoconference for free using

Skype. Going forward from this learning experience, I made concerted efforts to roll up my sleeves, learn alongside students and staff, and show my vested interest in being part of the change process, not just an empty suit barking out directives through impersonal means of communication.

Herein lay the missing piece to change, and that was the active process of modeling. When it comes to initiating sustainable change, educators must model the same expectations that they have of others. This is true for teachers and leaders alike. Setting a direction and helping people implement change are imperative for the successful implementation of any initiative. We must behave the same way they encourage others to behave, with their own voice and values by creating standards of excellence and then setting an example for others to follow (Kouzes & Posner, 2007). As they say, actions speak louder than words. Not only that, but we also learn by doing. As a leader I was in a better position to move a growth-based agenda forward as a result of not only modeling how to integrate technology effectively in a pedagogically sound fashion but also by demonstrating a willingness to learn.

Over time my teachers became the more significant catalyst for change as they began to learn on their own the many tools, strategies, and techniques that ultimately led to the transformation of our school learning culture, all of which will be discussed later in this book. As they began to implement effectively the purposeful integration of technology aligned to higher-order thinking skills, authentic work, and project-based learning, their actions served as models for their peers. The confidence of other teachers grew as they not only saw how their peers succeeded when implementing new ideas but also how they reacted to and overcame failure.

The importance of teachers modeling effective practices and the resulting impact should not come as a surprise. Almost all of us were immersed in the Madeline Hunter Model of Master Learning to develop pedagogically sound lessons and learning activities. Modeling was part of the basic vocabulary as it is important for students to see what they are learning, and it greatly helps them when the teacher demon-strates what is to be learned (Hunter, 1982). Move away from telling people what to do, and instead take them where they need to be. If you want change, model it. Modeling the way is one of the best things a leader can do to move others down a different path to initiate and sustain change.

REMOVE FEAR OF FAILURE, PROMOTE RISK TAKING, AND EMPOWER OTHERS

I have not failed. I've just found 10,000 ways that won't work.

— Thomas Edison

Imagine if Thomas Edison succumbed to failure. If he had, one of the greatest inventions of all time, the lightbulb, might not have been invented. Or worse yet, another inno-vative genius would have come along around that time or shortly after and invented it him- or herself. In schools the dreaded "f" word continues to plague progress on numer-ous levels. As the education reform movement has gained steam, newly implemented evaluation systems and the pro-liferation of new-age standardized assessments have invoked fear among educators like never before. As noted in Chapter 1, this has now led to a monotonous cycle of instruction with the sole purpose of preparing students for the standardized tests that now determine job security for educators and administrators alike. The fear of failure has become the main driver of instructional practices that main-tain conformity, control, and the status quo. Thus an innova-tive school culture that students and educators yearn for becomes a pipe dream at best.

For many teachers there is also the fear that accompanies classroom observations and evaluations by administrators, especially when it comes to the integration of technology or implementing an innovative learning activity for the first time. I remember as a teacher how nervous I would get when an administrator announced that he or she was coming to observe me. Think about how nervous the teachers I observed as an administrator must have been as they, for the most part, never knew when I was coming to observe as the majority of our observations were unannounced. This nervousness leads to fear, and the fear chains us down to lessons and activities that are safe, redundant, and squarely focused on improving the metrics that we are now judged on. Educators should never feel or be put in positions where observations and evaluations are seen as an "I gotcha." On the contrary, these are opportunities to showcase learning strategies and techniques that provide students with essential skill sets to make them real-world ready. They are a time to shine and demonstrate how uncommon learning methodologies are reaching students like never before.

Culture shock is needed so that uncommon learning becomes the norm, not the exception. For this to happen the fear of failure must be removed, and the word *failure* itself needs to be viewed from a positive perspective. When referring back to the Edison quote, it is apparent that failing led to different pathways each time that aligned to the objective he had set, which was inventing the lightbulb. Schools need to establish a shared vision where failure is seen as the ultimate catalyst for learning. Where once a notorious negative for holding back progress and change, failure now becomes the most powerful driver of innovation. Schools that no longer view failure as a roadblock, but an opportunity to improve just like Edison, are the ones that have developed transformative learning cultures where change has been embraced.

Teachers have extraordinary leadership capabilities, and their leadership is a major untapped resource for our nation's schools (Barth, 1990). It is important not only for teachers to see themselves as leaders but also for administrators to create the conditions where these teacher leaders can thrive by pushing the envelope through calculated risk taking. With no risk comes no reward. Removing the fear of failure empowers teachers and administrators to take calculated risks. Conversely, teachers themselves need to be empowered to take those risks.

Empowerment is the process by which people gain control over their lives . . . a participation with others to achieve goals, an effort to gain access to resources, and some critical understanding of the sociopolitical environment in schools (Perkins & Zimmerman, 1995). The right culture provides the spark teachers need to pursue and implement innovative practices actively in the classroom. In this situation it is clear to teachers that they have the autonomy and support to be as innovative as they want. There is less of a focus on control and more on trust, which both lend themselves to the creation of a school culture molded by empowerment.

If teachers do not have the confidence to give up the need to control all aspects of learning, students will not be in a position to make attempts, fail, and then succeed. Thus students need to be empowered just as much as teachers. Students who feel empowered are more confident and exhibit more self-esteem. Confidence can increase a person's ability to think and cope with basic challenges. Self-esteem can increase feeling worthy and the ability to assert one's needs and wants (Branden, 1994). The student voice movement is one shining example of how our learners desperately want to be empowered to take control and have more ownership over their learning. A school culture that works better for kids seizes the opportunity to have students be active participants in the development of class routines, learning activities, and assessments. Nothing empowers students more to want to learn than exhibiting trust in their ability to be drivers in this process. Thus a crucial element of culture shock is that leaders, teachers, and all students are empowered to take risks without the fear of failure.

SUPPORT

The learning culture of a school will not change overnight, nor will it happen if the necessary support structures are not in place. It is important to plant the seeds for change, and only after careful attention will those seeds germinate into sustainable changes leading to cultural transformation. All of the necessary ingredients discussed in this chapter are vitally important, but support is what drives each of those ingredients into embedded components of school culture. Support comes in many forms after a certain amount of control is relinquished and a great sense of trust is imparted among students. Listening, patience, resilience, and determination all play roles as the road to change requires an exorbitant amount of energy.

Without sounding redundant and rehashing what has already been discussed in this chapter, there are four specific areas of support that are needed to ensure the elements previously discussed become realistic components of a school culture that works better for kids. These include time, professional learning, infrastructure, and resources. Teachers need time to innovate, try new things, and learn. Schools need to begin to think about ways to free up teachers from contractual noninstructional duties and meaningless meetings. One common practice we initiated at my school was granting teachers release time from their contractual days to observe other teachers in the building and visit local schools that were innovating. We also released both teachers and students from regularly scheduled classes to engage in learning activities that required videoconferencing during other times. Being flexible with time and not allowing it to dictate the learning day supports uncommon learning.

Pivotal to any change initiative is support in the form of professional learning. Many schools and districts are plagued by poorly implemented professional learning initiatives that are not relevant, are dictated by a one-size-fits-all approach, provide no follow-up, lack differentiation, or focus on numerous initiatives simultaneously. Teachers and administrators need and deserve quality professional learning experiences that are relevant, meaningful, and applicable to teaching students growing up in the digital age. Uncommon learning thrives when school systems develop the internal capacity to provide continuous, ongoing professional learning based on the unique needs and passions of all staff members. The idea here is to leverage the expertise of the practitioners at your fingertips who are finding success implementing innovative pedagogies and methodologies. This is then complemented with the support of staff to attend relevant learning experiences out of district at conferences and workshop where the latest learning techniques are on display.

Infrastructure continues to be a thorn in the side of schools across the country. However, we can no longer afford to keep kicking the can down the road during budget season. All students deserve ubiquitous access to technology so that we adequately prepare them for success in the real world. Providing wireless access to the Internet must be a priority. Once this is in place there are endless possibilities that become available to support and enhance learning. The next step is to tackle access to mobile learning devices through either bring your own device (BYOD) or 1:1 initiatives. Chapter 6 specifically focuses on the drivers needed to effectively integrate both BYOD and 1:1 initiatives. Support in these endeavors requires the fortitude to press forward in the face of an array of challenges. Referendums will have to be petitioned for and passed, money will have to be allocated in tight budgets to purchase needed technology, and capital improvement funds will need to be utilized to transform learning spaces that are outdated and useless.

Finally, teachers and administrators need resources. Local operating budgets at both district and school levels can go only so far in providing tools and other resources that are needed to support uncommon learning practices. Innovative schools don't give up when they can't get the resources they need. On the contrary, they find ways to acquire the necessary tools and resources their students need to prepare them to be college and career ready. There are three cost-effective ways to do this that won't cost a dime:

1. Begin to discover the plethora of free resources found online. The Internet provides a bounty of resources that

can be implemented immediately either to enhance professional practice or support student learning in more authentic ways.

2. Form partnerships with local and national businesses and organizations that have a vested interest in education. (See example on page 120.)

3. Apply for available grants to get technology resources in the hands of teachers and students, especially in underprivileged areas. These will not just fall into your lap, though. You must make the time to search them out and exhibit patience when filling out the tedious applications.

SUMMARY

The learning cultures of schools needs a shock if they are to support uncommon learning practices that are not only innovative but support rigorous learning leading to greater levels of student achievement. There should be no compromise when it comes to providing all learners with the skills to be college and career ready or even simply prepared to succeed in a world that is evolving at a feverish pace. Culture shock requires shared vision, effective communication, autonomy, empowerment, removing the fear of failure, promoting collaboration, risk taking, ownership of learning, modeling, flexibility, and support. With these essential elements in place, changes will become embedded components of a transformational school culture where uncommon learning is the norm, not the exception. The following chapters will focus on specific uncommon learning strategies that can be implemented and sustained using the strategies from this chapter.

Digital Learning Across the Curriculum

How can instruction powerfully drive a new kind of learning that not only meets standards but also equips students with the skills they need to excel in a new kind of society? We must define and scaffold an approach to teaching and learning that fuses the solid tenets of rigorous and relevant instruction with an exceptional, discerning application of digital tools. This is important more than ever as technology is being infused into schools at a rapid pace. In 2014 American schools bought $8.38 billion in software, digital content, or training and assessments at an annual increase of more than 5 percent from the year before (Murphy, 2015).

Digital learning has the potential to not only enhance pedagogy but also to increase achievement. Project Revolutionizing Education (RED) conducted a national survey of technology programs in 1,000 schools focusing on academic results and the financial implications of education technology. The findings showed that if effectively implemented, technology programs can lead to improved student achievement and significant return on investment (Project RED, 2015). When given access to appropriate technology used in thoughtful ways, all students—regardless of their respective backgrounds—can make substantial gains in learning and technological readiness (Darling-Hammond, Zielezinski, & Goldman, 2014).

Those schools that have focused on increasing student achievement through the positive integration of digital tools have made a broad pedagogical shift: they have focused on enhancing essential skill sets—communication, collaboration, creativity, media literacy, global connectedness, critical thinking, and problem solving—by putting real-world tools into the hands of students. These tools allow students to create artifacts of learning that demonstrate their conceptual mastery. This mastery is not only more individually defined, driven, and produced, but also it enhances students' ability to create and learn more ably in their culture by increasing their digital confidence and expertise. The instructional style that has benefitted them is not one of mandates, directives, and buy-in but one grounded in empowerment, support, and embracement as keys to sustainable change.

A Culture Moving in a Different (Better) Direction

Hershey Groff is a history teacher at New Milford High School (NMHS). He believes that incorporating digital tools to increase student engagement while working to develop and extend student competencies is necessary in today's classroom. Additionally, he considers utilizing social media, digital learning games, mobile devices, and interactive educational applications as essential in promoting a classroom environment where engagement and collaboration directly result in increased student achievement and academic performance. Digital tools—used strategically as varied formative and summative assessments—are media that allow students to demonstrate the skill sets they have learned and developed along with the content knowledge they have acquired. Digital learning allows his students a variety of ways to showcase what they have learned while allowing the choice of tools to best suit their individual needs (Groff, personal communication, 2014).

Some of the social media tools that Groff utilizes most frequently to assess students digitally include Twitter, Pinterest, Instagram, and blogs. Students often see their social media accounts as an extension of themselves and updating their information and communicating with peers as part of their daily routine. Incorporating social media into the daily lessons in class immediately increases student engagement and levels of collaboration. Students can move beyond the confines of the classroom to engage in activities that have real-world applications. Groff likes to use Twitter, so students can conduct virtual discussions and class debates with students across the country. He also likes to have students Tweet as historical figures and fictional characters, which also can be done through pictures on Instagram accounts. This is used as both an assessment tool as well as a means to promote engagement in the classroom (Groff, 2014).

As an extension of the students' digital learning portfolios, Groff is a strong proponent of using Pinterest as a classroom tool. He uses this popular social bookmarking site to curate content, connect classrooms, share resources, and archive student research and work. He has students use Pinterest to create digital web galleries to present material and research logs when conducting extended research projects. Groff does not stop there. Digital learning strategies made possible through the use of social media allow him to connect with and engage parents in the learning process. He uses social media to communicate with parents, display student work, and share resources, which also results in enhanced levels of engagement and student achievement.

Additionally, Groff uses digital learning tools that incorporate elements of graphic design. Tools such as infographics, digital story and comic generators, Webpage design programs, and digital time lines are all used in his class to promote learning with real-world applications. In place of the traditional class essay, Groff often uses infographic creators such as Piktochart and Infogr.am, which require students to present their research with written text, charts and graphs, and images. This allows students to be creative in how they demonstrate their learning and appeals to students who possess different learning styles. It also provides students freedom to choose how to present their material, resulting in higher levels of engagement and content mastery.

Recently Groff piloted a program with his classes, called Paperlet, where students could create digital stories that incorporate text, images, video, sounds, and narration. Students were able to create customized stories of historical fiction surrounding important events following the Revolutionary War. Additionally, he used comic creators such as Storybird, Chogger, and the Draw My Life app. He found particular success with Draw My Life, with which students could record themselves drawing on whiteboards and create time-lapse videos with story lines and narration. Groff also has had students create digital time lines using tools such as Tiki-Toki, which include images and videos along with traditional text boxes. Tools that incorporate elements of design provide students choice and allow them to develop real-world skills while increasing classroom engagement. Groff has a firm understanding that students need to own their learning as opposed to him controlling it.

TENETS OF DIGITAL LEARNING

Our students want to be creative and collaborate, utilize technology for learning, connect with their peers in other countries, understand the messages that media convey, and solve real-world problems. Schools and systems of education that do not embrace digital learning and place a high emphasis on standardization will always fail to resonate with our students. It only makes sense to harness the power of technology as a catalyst for authentic engagement and application of concepts among our learners. If schools allow students to use the digital-age tools that they are using on a routine basis outside their walls, chances are that they will find more relevancy and meaning in what they are learning.

Digital learning can best be described as follows:

> Digital learning is any instructional practice that effectively uses technology to strengthen a student's learning experience. It emphasizes high-quality instruction and provides access to challenging content, feedback through formative assessment, opportunities for learning anytime and anywhere, and individualized instruction to ensure all students reach their full potential to succeed in college and a career.
>
> Digital learning encompasses many different facets, tools, and applications to support and empower teachers and students, including online courses, blended or hybrid learning, or digital content and resources. Additionally, digital learning can be used for professional learning opportunities for teachers and to provide personalized learning experiences for students.
>
> Digital learning advances school reform by increasing equity and access to educational opportunities, improving effectiveness and productivity of teachers and administrators, providing student-centered learning to ensure college and career readiness for all students, and recognizing teachers as education designers. (Alliance for Excellent Education, 2014)

Digital learning requires a mind-set that unleashes the creativity of students so that they can create artifacts of learning that demonstrate conceptual mastery. It is about providing learners with the knowledge, skills, and confidence to succeed in college, careers, and jobs that have not even been created yet. This is accomplished by allowing students to use real-world tools to apply what they have learned and construct new knowledge. By focusing on how specific technologies can be used to engage students, educators begin to establish a foundation for learning that will lead to eventual increases in student achievement. This becomes a reality when school cultures are transformed to meet and anticipate the needs of learners in the digital age.

Initially it is not a stretch to transition from traditional learning methodologies to those that incorporate digital aspects as many of the same tenets that comprise sound pedagogy still apply. The main difference is the embracement of digital tools to support and enhance the learning that is and should be taking place. The main tenets of digital learning are as follows:

- Sound pedagogy: It is crucial that sound pedagogical techniques and best practices are emphasized to effectively integrate technology to enhance teaching and learning. One of the most important questions an educator needs to answer is how the students are using technology to apply learning and demonstrate conceptual mastery. Students must always be at the center of this process. All too often technology is infused into the learning environment where the teacher is still employing a direct approach to instruction. When developing lessons that incorporate digital aspects, always consider first and foremost how the technology will allow students to arrive at the prescribed learning outcomes. It is imperative that standards-aligned rubrics be developed by teachers to assess learning while providing students guidance on their advancement toward demonstrating the learning outcomes.
- Access: It is quite difficult to incorporate digital learning into daily lessons and across the curriculum if students do not have ubiquitous access to the Internet, web-based tools, and devices. Without access, digital learning becomes nothing but a pipe dream.
- Transparent assessment: Digital learning allows educators to transparently assess students in ways like never before. More challenging assessments can be developed where students use digital tools they select to best articulate what they have learned, along with

knowledge that has been constructed, and apply essential skills that have been recently acquired. With thousands of tools available and more becoming accessible each day, educators have more options to assess students formatively and summatively than ever before. With Google Docs teachers can provide real-time feedback to students as they write research papers. Blogs allow students to openly reflect on their learning, while comments from teachers and their peers provide feedback. There are also many web-based tools such as Poll Everywhere, Plickers, Kahoot, and TodaysMeet that can be integrated for formative assessment while giving every single student a voice. When integrating technology, always remember that it is less about the tool and more about what students can do with tools they chose to demonstrate what they have learned. Pedagogy always trumps technology. For digital learning to be implemented effectively, focus on pedagogy first and technology second when appropriate. Do not haphazardly throw technology into a lesson because it will address a required checkbox on an observation form. Do it with learning intent and purpose.

- **Contextual and relevant curriculum**: It is important that students not only experience relevancy in their learning but also see the interconnectedness of the various content areas they are exposed to each day. Digital learning methodologies allow students to explore essential concepts related to Common Core or specified state standards in deeper, more authentic ways to transform bland curriculum into learning experiences in which students find value. A contextual curriculum supported by pedagogy promotes inquiry, creates a supportive learning environment, encourages reflection, enhances the relevance of new learning, facilitates collaboration, invokes communication, allows students to actively solve real-world problems, makes connections to prior learning and experiences, and provides sufficient opportunities to learn through choice and application. Digital learning provides a natural link to not only add context that students deserve but the relevancy they expect.

- **Essential skill sets**: Digital learning should promote the acquisition, enhancement, and application of essential skill sets that students will need to succeed in a rapidly changing world. The inherent and intuitive nature of

Figure 3.1

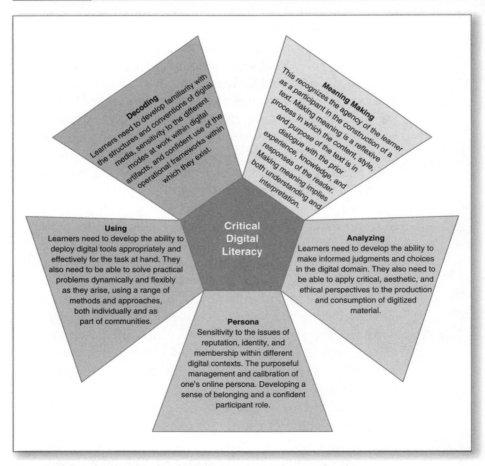

Source: TeachThought (2014). Developed by Juliet Hinrichsen and Antony Coombs.

Figure 3.2

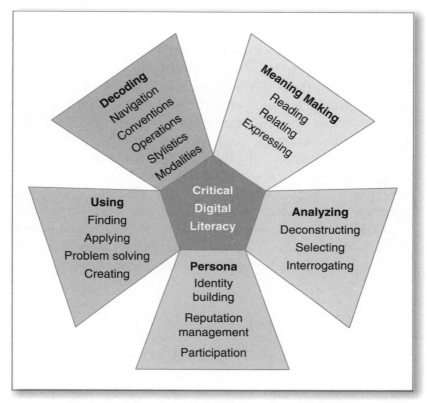

Source: TeachThought (2014). Developed by Juliet Hinrichsen and Antony Coombs.

many digital tools seamlessly works to foster communication, collaboration, creativity, entrepreneurship, critical thinking and problem-solving skills, online responsibility, and core literacies for the digital age. These skill sets are described in detail in Appendix B. Higher standards across the country, whether in the form of Common Core or revamped state standards, place a heavy emphasis on literacy. Digital learning not only promotes traditional literacies but also vital literacies prevalent in a technologically advanced society. These critical digital literacies include decoding, meaning making, analyzing, persona, and using (TeachThought, 2014).

FRAMEWORKS TO GUIDE
SUCCESSFUL IMPLEMENTATION

There are several learning frameworks and tools that educators should be aware of to assist with the transition to and effective integration of technology to support learning. Without learning activities grounded in sound pedagogy and the proper support structures in place, technology in the classroom becomes nothing but a bells-and-whistles approach to increasing student engagement while having no positive impact on learning. Technology must be integrated with purpose and aligned to the construction of new knowledge, application to demonstrate conceptual mastery, or acquisition of new skills that students need to compete in the real world. Uncommon learning supports the notion that technology facilitates deeper, more authentic learning to address higher standards being adopted across the globe.

SAMR

Substitution Augmentation Modification Redefinition (SAMR), developed by Dr. Ruben Puentedura, is a framework that provides a method of observing how educational technology will facilitate the teaching and learning process. It articulates a progression that teachers commonly employ when they integrate new technologies to support teaching and learning. There is room for constructive dialogue as to whether one particular activity can be described as one level or another; however, the important concept to understand is the impact on authentic student engagement and learning supporting a defined learning outcome. As a teacher travels along the continuum, technology becomes a more embedded component of the learning activity. The further along an educator travels down the continuum represents the effective integration of technology to support and enhance student learning.

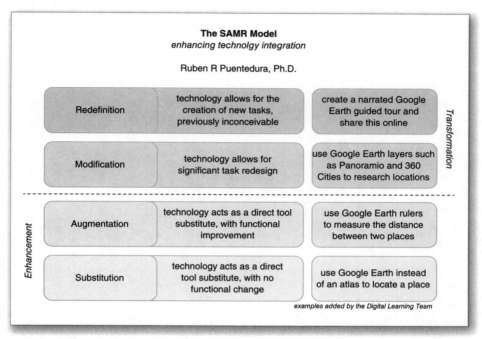

Figure 3.3

The SAMR Model
enhancing technolgy integration

Ruben R Puentedura, Ph.D.

Redefinition	technology allows for the creation of new tasks, previously inconceivable	create a narrated Google Earth guided tour and share this online
Modification	technology allows for significant task redesign	use Google Earth layers such as Panoramio and 360 Cities to research locations
Augmentation	technology acts as a direct tool substitute, with functional improvement	use Google Earth rulers to measure the distance between two places
Substitution	technology acts as a direct tool substitute, with no functional change	use Google Earth instead of an atlas to locate a place

Transformation

Enhancement

examples added by the Digital Learning Team

Source: Puentedura (2012)

TPACK

Technological Pedagogical Content Knowledge (TPACK) is a framework that identifies the knowledge teachers should possess to integrate technology effectively in the classroom. The framework outlines the interconnectedness of three primary forms of knowledge: content (CK), pedagogy (PK), and technology (TK). TPACK extends beyond viewing these different types of knowledge in isolation. It also places an emphasis on emerging types of knowledge that lie at the intersections between them, representing four more knowledge bases teachers can apply to pedagogy that incorporates technology: pedagogical content knowledge (PCK), technological content knowledge (TCK), technological pedagogical knowledge

Table 3.1

Level	Definition	Examples	Functional Change
Substitution	Technology is used to perform the same task as was done before, where it represents a direct substitute.	Teacher has students complete a paper or digital worksheet.	There is no functional change, and many times teachers use technology to complete the same task that could have been completed without it. Technology does not advance learning or provide any added benefits. More often than not these activities are teacher centered.
Augmentation	Technology acts as a direct tool substitute, with functional improvement.	Students are formatively or summatively assessed using a digital tool (i.e., Quizlet, Google Form) instead of using pencil and paper.	Some functional change results with the shift from paper to digital. The digital tools provide at times immediate feedback to students. The timely feedback informs students about their progress toward meeting the learning outcomes while increasing engagement.
Modification	Technology allows for significant task redesign to transform teaching and learning.	Students are asked to write an informative essay on the effect the Great Depression had on people who lived through it while providing textual evidence to support their thinking.	There is significant functional change in the classroom. While all students are learning similar writing skills, the reality of an authentic audience gives each student a personal stake in the quality of the work.

Level	Definition	Examples	Functional Change
(Modification)	(Technology allows for significant task redesign to transform teaching and learning.)	A multimedia product using technology is created, as well as shown, in front of an authentic live audience or shared online using social media tools.	Computer technology is necessary for this classroom to function, allowing peer and teacher feedback, easy rewriting, and audio recording. Questions about writing skills increasingly come from the students themselves.
Redefintion	Technology allows for creation of new tasks, previously inconceivable.	Students are given a choice as to what technology tool they want use to create a product that answers an essential question related to important concepts. Students collaborate to create an artifact. Students are expected to research and cite sources appropriately and also ensure that technology can be used to share their projects across an array of social networks.	Here the teacher becomes more of a facilitator in a truly student-centered environment. Students are empowered to take ownership of their learning while developing critical media literacies. As drivers of their own learning, students begin to experience a more contextual curriculum that builds relevancy. Technology is used to showcase conceptual understanding in ways not previously imagined or promoted.

(TPK), and the intersection of all three circles, Technological Pedagogical Content Knowledge (TPACK).

Effective technology integration for pedagogy around specific subject matters requires developing sensitivity to the dynamic, transactional relationships among these components of knowledge situated in unique contexts. Individual teachers, grade levels, school-specific factors, demographics, culture, and other factors ensure that every situation is unique and no single combination of content, technology, and pedagogy will apply for every teacher, every course, or every view of teaching (Mishra & Koehler, 2006).

The TPACK framework can be a bit confusing for teachers in terms of determining how it can be applied to ensure the effective integration of technology to support learning. Mathew Koehler (2012) provides the following details:

- **Content Knowledge (CK):** "Teachers' knowledge about the subject matter to be learned or taught. The content to be covered in middle school science or history is different from the content to be covered in an undergraduate course on art appreciation or a graduate seminar on astrophysics . . . As Shulman (1986) noted, this knowledge would include knowledge of concepts, theories, ideas, organizational frameworks, knowledge of evidence and proof, as well as established practices and approaches toward developing such knowledge" (Koehler & Mishra, 2009).
- **Pedagogical Knowledge (PK):** "Teachers' deep knowledge about the processes and practices or methods of teaching and learning. They encompass, among other things, overall educational purposes, values, and aims. This generic form of knowledge applies to understanding how students learn, general classroom management skills, lesson planning, and student assessment" (Koehler & Mishra, 2009).
- **Technology Knowledge (TK):** "Knowledge about certain ways of thinking about, and working with technology, tools and resources and working with technology

can apply to all technology tools and resources. This includes understanding information technology broadly enough to apply it productively at work and in everyday life, being able to recognize when information technology can assist or impede the achievement of a goal, and being able continually adapt to changes in information technology" (Koehler & Mishra, 2009).

- **Pedagogical Content Knowledge (PCK):** "Consistent with and similar to Shulman's idea of knowledge of pedagogy that is applicable to the teaching of specific content. Central to Shulman's conceptualization of PCK is the notion of the transformation of the subject matter for teaching. Specifically, according to Shulman (1986), this transformation occurs as the teacher interprets the subject matter, finds multiple ways to represent it, and adapts and tailors the instructional materials to alternative conceptions and students' prior knowledge. PCK covers the core business of teaching, learning, curriculum, assessment and reporting, such as the conditions that promote learning and the links among curriculum, assessment, and pedagogy" (Koehler & Mishra, 2009).

- **Technological Content Knowledge (TCK):** "An understanding of the manner in which technology and content influence and constrain one another. Teachers need to master more than the subject matter they teach; they must also have a deep understanding of the manner in which the subject matter (or the kinds of representations that can be constructed) can be changed by the application of particular technologies. Teachers need to understand which specific technologies are best suited for addressing subject-matter learning in their domains and how the content dictates or perhaps even changes the technology—or vice versa" (Koehler & Mishra, 2009).

- **Technological Pedagogical Knowledge (TPK):** "An understanding of how teaching and learning can change when particular technologies are used in particular ways. This includes knowing the pedagogical affordances and constraints of a range of technological tools as they relate to disciplinarily and developmentally appropriate pedagogical designs and strategies" (Koehler & Mishra, 2009).

- **Technological Pedagogical Content Knowledge (TPACK):** "Underlying truly meaningful and deeply skilled teaching with technology, TPACK is different from knowledge of all three concepts individually. Instead, TPACK is the basis of effective teaching with technology, requiring an understanding of the representation of concepts using technologies; pedagogical techniques that use technologies in constructive ways to teach content; knowledge of what makes concepts difficult or easy to learn and how technology can help redress some of the problems that students face; knowledge of students' prior knowledge and theories of epistemology; and knowledge of how technologies can be used to build on existing knowledge to develop new epistemologies or strengthen old ones" (Koehler & Mishra, 2009).

Technology Integration Matrix

The Technology Integration Matrix (TIM) was created by the Florida Center for Instructional Technology at the University of South Florida. The first iteration of this tool was developed in 2005 and 2006 with an updated, interactive version released in 2011. This framework provides teachers with an array of clear indicators on how they can use technology to enhance learning for students at all grade levels. Embedded within the tool are five interdependent characteristics of relevant learning environments. These include active, constructive, goal directed, authentic, and collaborative. The TIM associates five levels of technology integration (i.e., entry, adoption, adaptation, infusion, and transformation) with each of the five characteristics of relevant learning environments. All in all, the five levels of technology integration

Figure 3.4

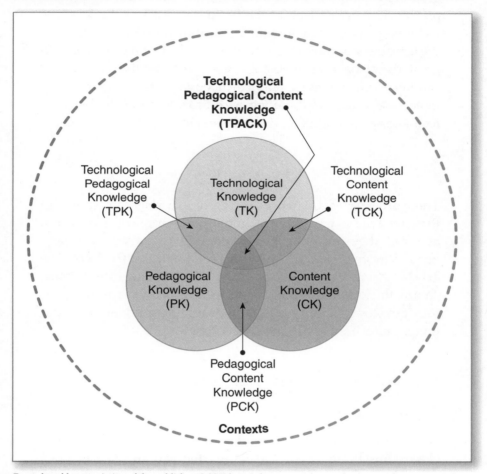

and the five characteristics of relevant learning environments create a matrix of 25 cells, which can be accessed at fcit.usf .edu/matrix/matrix.php.

When accessing this interactive version of TIM, educators can dive deep into each of the cells to view clear indicators for each. The main page also allows anyone to see sample lessons in math, English language arts (ELA), social studies, and science.

These allow educators to clearly see the level of technology integration in relation to student learning and outcomes. By clicking on the right arrow icon at the bottom of each of the levels of technology integration into the curriculum and characteristics of the learning environment, educators will be taken to a page with great detail on each element. Descriptors for typical teacher activity, student activity, and instructional settings are included in each separate matrix along with links to all of the levels of technology integration and characteristic video lesson pages.

A Better Process

There are many frameworks out there to assist educators with the effective integration of technology to support learning, but at times they are not concrete enough to provide a much-needed focus that educators yearn for. Enter the Trudacot. The Trudacot was developed by Scott McLeod and Julie Graber. Taking the foundational elements from an array of frameworks, they developed a tool focused on providing guidance to better integrate technology in the classroom.

The Trudacot

(Adapted with permission from McLeod and Graber)

We have a lot of technology floating around our schools and classrooms these days. And while that can and should be a good thing given the digital age in which we now live, we often find that our technology-related efforts aren't paying off for us as we had hoped. For example, we see a lot of replicative use—doing the same things that we used to do in analog classrooms, only with more expensive tools—and we see many teachers using technology simply for technology's sake. There are many reasons why all of this is true, but a primary one is that we don't have great ways to think about what is occurring when we see students and teachers using technology for learning and teaching purposes.

TPACK and SAMR are the two main technology integration frameworks being used right now. While conceptually useful, both of them have their limitations. For instance, neither is very specific when it comes to helping teachers think about *what to change* to make their technology integration better. The SAMR levels have the additional challenge of apparently meaning very different things to different people; we have witnessed on numerous occasions a particular usage of technology placed in all four SAMR levels by educator audiences. Resources like the TPACK activity types help with some of this, but we were looking for something different. Failing to find what we wanted, we decided to make our own. *Technology-Rich Unit Design And Classroom Observation Template (Trudacot) is a protocol intended to help facilitate educator conversations about deeper learning, student agency, and technology integration.*

Starting With Purpose

Technology integration should be purposeful. That very simple statement is at the heart of the Trudacot template. When we use digital technologies for learning and teaching, those uses should be intentional and targeted, not simply tech for tech's sake. Our team continually asks the question, "Technology for the purpose of what?" With that in mind, we set out to create a template of questions that would allow educators to think critically—and purposefully—about their technology integration.

For example, if a class activity was using learning technologies for the purpose of enhancing personalization or enabling greater student agency and choice, the types of questions that we would ask to see might include the following:

- *Learning Goals.* Who selected what is being learned?
- *Learning Activity.* Who selected how it is being learned?
- *Assessment of Learning.* Who selected how students demonstrate their knowledge and skills and how that will be assessed?

- *Work Time.* During the lesson or unit, who is the primary driver of the work time?
- *Technology Usage.* Who is the primary user of the technology?

In contrast, if teachers wanted students to use technology for the purpose of enabling them to do more authentic, real-world work, the types of questions that we would ask to see would be different from those previous and might include the following:

- *Real or Fake.* Is student work authentic and reflective of that done by real people outside of school?
- *Domain Knowledge.* Are students learning discipline-specific and appropriate content and procedural knowledge? If yes, is student work focused around big, important concepts central to the discipline (not just minutiae)?
- *Domain Practices.* Are students utilizing discipline-specific and appropriate practices and processes?
- *Domain Technologies.* Are students utilizing discipline-specific and appropriate tools and technologies?

Similarly, if a lesson or unit integrated learning technologies for the purpose of facilitating students' deeper thinking, creativity, or metacognition, the types of questions that we would ask to see might include the following:

- *Deeper Thinking.* Do student learning activities and assessments go beyond facts, procedures, or previously provided ways of thinking (e.g., syntheses or analyses that actually are regurgitations)?
- *Creativity.* Do students have the opportunity to design, create, make, or otherwise add value that is unique to them?
- *Initiative.* Do students have the opportunity to initiate, be entrepreneurial, be self-directed, or go beyond given parameters of the learning task or environment?

- *Metacognition.* Do students have the opportunity to reflect on their planning, thinking, work, or progress? If yes, can students identify what they're learning, not just what they're doing?

The Trudacot tries to get at some specific, concrete "look-fors" that can help educators think about what they might change. In other words, we are attempting with Trudacot to make explicit the kinds of questions we might ask when considering which intersection of TPACK—or level of SAMR—a particular instance of technology integration may be inhabiting (and how to shift it toward more robustness).

Using Trudacot

Version 2 of Trudacot is now available and includes annotations and tips for usage. First and foremost is the suggestion to focus on just one or two sections of the template. Unless we're designing a big, multi-week project, we need to pick and choose a few focal areas rather than trying to cover the entire template. Let us be clear: the Trudacot template should *not* be used as a massive checklist of things that should be present in a teacher's lesson or unit. A second suggestion is to answer a question or two from Trudacot about a lesson or unit—preferably in small groups, not just individually—and then ask, "If we wanted the answer(s) to the question(s) to be different, how could we redesign this to make that desired answer happen instead?" This is where the powerful conversations occur; this is the work we should be doing with educators. Finally, we are finding Trudacot to have the most power as an up-front brainstorming, idea-generating, and design tool, not an after-the-fact evaluative tool. We want educators thinking about lesson and unit (re)design in ways that are safe and generative, not worrying about being judged. One great way to do this is to first use Trudacot to look at lessons that are not our own to minimize educators' defensiveness.

In addition to the Trudacot itself, we have numerous other resources and examples of Trudacot in practice. We hope that you find Trudacot useful to your own technology integration efforts and that it helps you foster rich discussions about lesson and unit (re)design with your educators. Please stay in touch as you have questions, ideas, and suggestions; we are happy to set up online meetings with you to explain Trudacot further. The Trudacot template is very much a work in progress—help us make it better! The more people that we have looking at and working with Trudacot, the more useful it can become. The Trudacot can be accessed digitally at http://dangerouslyirrelevant.org/resources/trudacot or http://bit.ly/trudacot (McLeod & Graber, personal communication, 2015).

THE RIGOR AND RELEVANCE FRAMEWORK

The Rigor and Relevance Framework—an action-oriented continuum that describes putting knowledge to use—gives teachers a way to develop both instruction and assessment and gives students a way to project learning goals. This framework, based on traditional elements of education yet encouraging movement from *acquisition* of knowledge to *application* of knowledge, charts learning along the two dimensions of higher standards and student achievement.

Capable teacher presence and teacher-centered instruction always belong in the foreground and always underpin lasting student learning, no matter what digital tools are in use. Grounded in rigor and relevance, instruction and learning with digital tools are limitless.

Student Learning and Achievement in the Digital Age

Learning must always be relevant, meaningful, and applicable. Student engagement is a bedrock necessity of attentive and deep learning. Excitement about academic growth, in

Figure 3.5

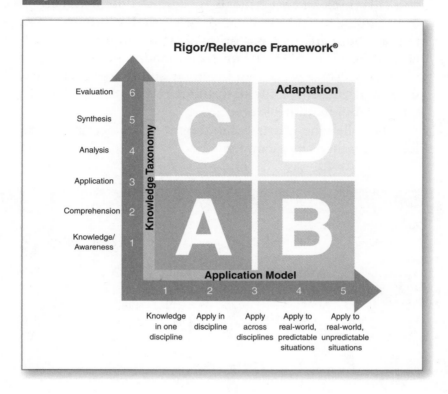

turn, drives increased student achievement, not only in terms of meeting and exceeding standards but also in terms of learning that extends into all realms of life. With the solid pedagogical foundation that the Rigor and Relevance Framework provides, digital tools and social media afford students the opportunity to take more ownership of their growth and development. Allowing students choice over which tools they will use to create artifacts of their learning that demonstrate conceptual mastery builds a greater appreciation for learning while simultaneously preparing them for the real world.

With advanced digital tools under their belts, students grow to develop their own learning tasks—such as podcasting, blogging, or digitally storytelling—that stretch their creativity, originality, design, or adaptation. These students think and act critically to curate content and apply information to address a range of cross-disciplinary tasks that are both creative and original. This could include collaborating with others using social media, networking, or reviewing. Their work requires their ability to select, organize, and present content through relevant digital tools, which provide multiple solutions.

The following charts break down and categorize digital tools and actions by quadrant.

Quadrant C	
• Editing • Hyperlinking • Media Clipping/Cropping • Monitoring • Photos/Videos • Programming	• Reverse Engineering • Software Cracking • Testing • Validating Resources

Quadrant D	
• Animating • Audio Casting • Blog Comments • Broadcasting • Collaborating • Composing • Digital Storytelling • Directing	• Mashing and Mixing/Remixing • Networking • Photo/Video Blogging • Podcasting • Reviewing

Quadrant A	
• Bullets and Lists • Creating and Naming Folders • Editing • Highlight Selecting	• Internet Searching • Loading • Typing • Using a Mouse • Word Doc

Quadrant B	
• Advanced Searching • Annotating • Blogs • Google Docs • Operating/Running a Program • Posting—Social Media	• Replying and Commenting • Sharing • Social Bookmarking • Subscribing to RSS Feed • Tagging • Texting • Uploading • Web Authoring

How Do These Categories Align to the Four Quadrants of the Rigor and Relevance Framework?

The skills in each quadrant are grouped in progression from basic to advanced, with the foundational skills in Quadrants A and B setting up the integrative and advanced skills in Quadrants C and D.

Quadrant A skills provide basic knowledge of digital and social media. Students gather knowledge or recognize their existing knowledge, demonstrating understanding of the purpose and outcome each skill provides.

Quadrant B skills are those that show the student's ability to apply his or her acquired knowledge in digital and social media: to solve problems, design solutions, and complete work. The skills at the end of the list will challenge students to apply their knowledge to new and unpredictable situations.

Quadrant C skills describe those that digitally capable students have mastered. These skills show an extension and refinement of acquired knowledge and an ability to solve problems and create solutions in predictable situations.

Quadrant D skills are those that apply to real-world, unpredictable situations. These skills mark the ability to use digital tools and social media to think in complex ways and to be the author of understanding in the digital world.

The Rigor and Relevance Framework, when coupled with literacy in digital and social tools, frees teachers and students to do much more than just meet standards. It liberates them into an understanding of growth that gives students relevance and positions them to be owners of their knowledge and members of their world.

Applying Digital Tools

How can we create pathways for rigorous and relevant use of digital tools? These best practices can help:

1. Prioritize Instructional Excellence

Technology can be an effective tool, but it remains just that, a tool. Educators provide the backbone of the student's learning experience. A teacher should always have concrete answers to these questions:

- What capabilities do I want my students to develop? In what specific ways is my instructional design rigorous, relevant, and goal oriented?
- What are my benchmarks for rigor? Relevance? Relationships? Clear objectives?

With these responses, teachers and students can then consider a specific digital tool, asking the following:

- How does this digital tool support the development of the capability I want to develop in my students?
- Is my teaching, using this tool, still as structured, rigorous, and relevant as it would be without this tool?

2. Identify Student Needs Around Use of Digital Tools

Information should not be confused with knowledge of evaluating digital tools. Knowledge is the recall of information, discovery, observation, or naming. Teachers should be able to define what knowledge (not information) students will need to apply when using a digital tool.

3. Create a Game Plan for Managing Student Use of Online Tools

It takes work and careful planning to implement the use of digital tools in defined ways. Before introducing a digital tool into a learning context, teachers should understand the following:

- How they will be able to support students in using a tool that might be unfamiliar
- How each student will be able to manage it independently
- How they will take advantage of students' diversity and inclination toward building community online
- How students and instructor will connect across sometimes great distance

4. Maximize Opportunities for Diverse Forms of Feedback

Rather than relying on feedback or evaluation models suited to outdated models of assignments, have teachers ask these questions:

- How will this online tool allow me to home in on each student's thought process and provide targeted, formative feedback that can be immediately and usefully applied?
- How can my feedback help pave the way for next steps in learning and in reaching established, articulated, or modeled goals?

Five Steps Toward Building Successful Digital Communities Infused With Rigor and Relevance

A dynamic combination of mind-set, behaviors, and skills is required for schools to become places where social media and digital tools are integral and beneficial parts of a rigorous program and where they work symbiotically with active, engaged, and applicable learning.

How can we take the greatest advantage of this moment in time and create compelling and challenging learning spaces for students? The most important things to do are to give up control and to trust students and their teachers to use real-world tools to unleash creativity and a passion for learning. After putting these tenets in the foundation, the specifics can take several different forms:

Step 1: Realize that social media is a predominant tool in the world. It fosters personalization, creativity, and collaboration, giving students infinite ways in which to create artifacts of their learning and knowledge.

Step 2: Make use of devices students already have, know, and use. Bring your own device (BYOD) signals to kids that teachers know and understand their basic makeup.

Employing the energy surrounding personal devices allows them to use the tools that help them do what they do better. BYOD enhances learning, increases productivity, allows students to grow their research skills, and gives teachers the chance to teach appropriate digital responsibility.

Step 3: Create spaces for making, collaborating, and tinkering. Give students chances to build and create using real-world tools (woodshop, electronics, metal work, and coding stations) and solve open-ended, real-world problems. Bring play back into the picture. These spaces provide students with challenging problems to solve where there is no one correct solution. Through self-directed learning, students are driven to find solutions to create a product that has value.

Step 4: Structure schools so that they more accurately reflect the real world. Ubiquitous connectivity, charging stations, and casual zones that promote conversation and play increase students' sense of belonging and engagement. Digitally astute students engage through such models as blended learning, flipped classrooms, games, makerspaces, and virtual learning.

Step 5: Give students access to open courseware and open source technology. Inherent in these approaches is a high level of choice about what to focus on, which in turn leads to greater ownership over learning and personalized ways to demonstrate understanding.

Ambitious, successful teaching and learning have become inherently intertwined with the digital world. Educators must be able to develop and enact rigorous, relevant instructional methods and formats while using digital tools effectively to underpin their instruction. Students and teachers can transform learning so that it not only prepares them to excel in academic life but also endows them with essential digital age skills.

ENGAGEMENT DOES NOT
ALWAYS EQUATE TO LEARNING

No matter where I am, whether it is a physical location or virtual, I am always hearing conversations about how technology can be used to engage students effectively. This is extremely important as the majority of students spend six to eight hours a day in schools where they are completely disengaged. I for one can't blame today's learner for being bored in school when I all have to do is observe my own son at home playing Minecraft to see firsthand his high level of engagement. His Minecraft experiences provide meaning and relevance in an environment that is intellectually stimulating but, more importantly, fun. Schools and educators would be wise to take cues from the real world and make concerted efforts to integrate technology with the purpose to increase student engagement. Engagement, after all, is the impetus for learning in my opinion.

Hidden Curriculum (2014) provides the following definition of engagement:

> In education, student engagement refers to the degree of attention, curiosity, interest, optimism, and passion that students show when they are learning or being taught, which extends to the level of motivation they have to learn and progress in their education. Generally speaking, the concept of "student engagement" is predicated on the belief that learning improves when students are inquisitive, interested, or inspired, and that learning tends to suffer when students are bored, dispassionate, disaffected, or otherwise "disengaged." Stronger student engagement or improved student engagement are common instructional objectives expressed by educators.

The last line in this description elicits a great deal of concern for me. With or without technology, there always seems to be a great deal of emphasis on student engagement, but the fact of the matter is that engagement does not necessarily equate to learning. I have observed numerous lessons where students were obviously engaged through the integration of technology, but there was no clear indication that students were learning. Having fun, collaborating, communicating, and being creative are all very important elements that should be embedded elements of pedagogically sound lessons, but we must not lose sight of the importance of the connection to, and evidence of, learning. Thus, students can walk away from a lesson or activity having been very engaged but with very little in the form of new knowledge construction, conceptual mastery, or evidence of applied skills. When speaking at events I often ask leaders and teachers how they measure the impact of technology on learning. More often than not I receive blank stares or an open admission that they have no idea. The allure of engagement can be blinding as well as misleading.

It is so important to look beyond mere student engagement when it comes to technology. If the emphasis is on digital learning, we must not get caught up in the bells and whistles or smoke and mirrors that are commonly associated with the digital aspect alone. Engagement should always translate into deeper learning opportunities where technology provides students the means to think critically and solve problems while demonstrating what they know and can do in a variety of ways. Technology should be implemented to increase engagement, but that engagement must lead to support, enhancement, or an increase in student learning. It should not be used as a digital pacifier or gimmick to get students to be active participants in class. With technology there should be a focus on active learning where students are doing.

Here are some questions that will assist in determining if engagement is leading to actual learning:

- Is the technology being integrated in a purposeful way, grounded in sound pedagogy?
- What are the learning objectives or outcomes?
- Are students demonstrating the construction of new knowledge? Are they creating a learning product or artifact?

- How are students applying essential skills they have acquired to demonstrate conceptual mastery?
- What assessments (formative or summative) are being used to determine standard attainment?
- How are students being provided feedback about their progress toward the specific learning objectives or outcomes?
- Is there alignment to current observation or evaluation tools?

Engagement, relevance, and fun are great, but make sure there is observable evidence that students are learning when integrating technology.

A Shining Example

In 2006 Mrs. Joanna Westbrook left the United States for a three-year stint overseas to teach in international schools in both Europe and Africa. At the time, she was leaving a South Carolina high school that was, by today's measures, technologically disadvantaged. Her students had no real computer access with only a lab for word processing and a bank of computers in the library to use for research. In her instruction, she had students use technology as a way to retrieve information and type papers rather than as a way to interact with information. But when she began teaching in an international school with one-to-one technology, she had to change how she saw technology use in ELA. Every student in every single one of Mrs. Westbrook's classes now had a MacBook, and students exhibited ease with technology that sparked the first shift in her teaching. It was a heady time. Suddenly, she had gone from a school that was tech impoverished to a school that was tech privileged. Her students had instant access to information. She was able to provide more timely feedback by inserting comments and tracking changes in their drafts. Students researched quickly and accessed relevant visuals that came up in discussion.

Mrs. Westbrook began to see what current technology could do to enhance her teaching. But unfortunately she also slowly began to see what technology couldn't do.

The way Mrs. Westbrook integrated technology certainly shifted her teaching, but it didn't result in a corresponding improvement in her kids' learning. As she worked with students more and more, she came to the hard realization that though she had *access* to all the bells and whistles of modern technology for her students, her *use* of technology had become the goal of some lessons. Thus what she was doing with the technology was not really helping students learn more about the content. She even began to feel that her students were using their computers as a crutch or a shortcut.

> Whether the result of my own inexperience or from a lack of real administrative support, I felt that the way I used technology became an obstacle to deeper learning in my classroom. I need to think about technology in a *deeper* way in order for my students to use technology in a *smarter* way. I just needed to figure out what *smarter* meant. (Westbrook, personal communication, 2014)

"Then in 2012 my technology work was enhanced even further by my move to New Milford High School and the support of my principal Eric Sheninger" (Westbrook, 2014). NMHS was a BYOD school where her students had ample access to technology. More importantly, however, is that teachers had ample administrative support to integrate technology and social media. Administrative support and like-minded colleagues sparked a second shift in her teaching when she realized that while she had been capitalizing on the fact that technology gave her more access points to student thought, she had failed to capitalize on the fact that the content discourse of ELA instruction mirrors discourse of social media. Instead of focusing on access to technology, she shifted her focus to the purposeful use of technology for real interaction with content.

For example, Mrs. Westbook used TodaysMeet (www .todaysmeet.com), a back channel for gathering student feedback and commentary. TodaysMeet works just like Twitter in that questions and responses are limited to 140 characters and students can post comments online during live conversation. But it differs from Twitter in that the audience is limited to the students who have the link, allowing Mrs. Westbrook to control the duration and participants of each post. This feature both protects and focuses students. Using TodaysMeet helps her counteract the limitations of traditional classroom discussion where often the same few students dominate the discussion, allowing some students to fade into the background. In addition, the comments on TodaysMeet can be archived, allowing her students to revisit the conversations and use the ideas to drive subsequent discussions. "The back channel provides a means for students to participate in our classroom conversation while giving me insight into their learning at various points in the lesson. Each student participates and, therefore, each student also loses the ability to tune out" (Westbrook, 2014). These interactions allowed her to meet students where they were and raised the level of discourse as they wrestled with meaning and ideas embedded in a text. In this moment, social media provided her with a springboard to launch other lessons.

In addition, as students worked to master the complex reading and writing standards demanded by the Common Core, Mrs. Westbrook used blogging in her writing instruction. Like the back channel, blogging encourages authentic engagement. "I was introduced to Edublogs at New Milford and now set up a class blog for each of my classes at the beginning of each year. Edublogs allows me to create digital text sets, to pose questions for student reflection, and to create scaffolds for students to use as resources in their writing" (Westbrook, 2014). On the blog, she would post questions that grew out of the academic discourse of the unit of study. The class would discuss and write about real issues that arose from the reading. She was then able to moderate student responses and interactions as they posted their comments and received feedback from their classmates. Students saw their classmates struggle and reflect. The writing became a transparent process, and as a result, students learned from each other. Therefore, the class blog allowed Mrs. Westbrook to engage students in class discussion and in academic writing and to respond to them in ways that refined their thinking. In addition, she saw evidence of what each student was learning and where each student needed support while addressing the whole class. Finally, all of their writing is public. As students post, they generate a rich resource of exemplars that become models in subsequent formative assessments. "I believe using the opportunity the blogs give me to provide targeted feedback and support is one of the most powerful things I can do as a teacher. Students can then respond to the feedback immediately as they struggle to improve their writing, and I can help them when they don't know where and how to start" (Westbrook, 2014).

Purposeful Integration of Technology

For Mrs. Westbrook and teachers across the world, the definition of literacy is expanding. Students are reading and producing different kinds of texts. Using social media to increase student analysis of great literature helps them make sense of difficult text and make sense of their own reactions to the ideas and truths about human experience embedded in the text. For example, she wanted to incorporate Twitter into a unit on *Julius Caesar*. To begin she capitalized on the link between social interactions in Roman public life and her students' interactions on social media. But they weren't just using Twitter to fulfill a technology requirement in lesson planning. The content drove their choice. Mrs. Westbrook and her colleagues wanted to use a modern medium with which their students had facility to engage them more deeply in the ideas in the literature. In other words, they wanted their students to use social media for an academic purpose. In addition, NMHS ELA teachers also used Twitter as a mentor text for analyzing rhetoric. In their study of *Julius Caesar*, they targeted the power of diction, allusion, and juxtaposition. To reinforce those ideas, they tied Shakespeare's rhetoric to the rhetoric of Twitter very clearly.

To begin, the class read a nonfiction piece that linked contemporary social media to the social interactions in ancient Rome. As they read the piece, students annotated any characteristic of Roman discourse that connected or shared similarities to the type of discourse they had seen on Twitter. The argument the author of the article made was easily accessible to the students as they quickly connected the frequency of the written interactions in Rome to their own daily Tweeting and described the copying of correspondence from one person to the other as *reTweeting*. The article also grounded the class's use of social media to historical discourse and academic content. "By connecting the medium with the content so plainly, we gave students a context and purpose for using Twitter with this particular play and in this particular way" (Westbrook, 2014).

The next step for Mrs. Westbrook's class was to differentiate the process by analyzing the rhetoric of Twitter. To scaffold that process, she asked students to generate a list of the types of Tweets they saw in their daily lives. They then talked through those examples of the rhetoric of Twitter such as Twitter fights, memes, reTweets, and updates. In addition, the class identified and analyzed the visual rhetoric of sample Twitter pages focusing on the intended effect of the author's choices on the audience for the page. They noted the importance of the content of header photos, profile photos, and the written profile in presenting character. As a result, students were given more than one reference point and more than one access point to literacy content. Finally, they worked with Laura Fleming, the digital media specialist, to find a way to help students use memes to improve the content of their Tweets. As a result the class used a Mozilla Webmaker tool called Mozilla Thimble to create memes. Thimble allowed students to create and share their own web-based memes edited right in their browsers. This step allowed both the tech-savvy and non-tech-savvy students to present their visuals in a more professional manner and brought visual clarity and some humor and creativity to their responses. A description of the learning activity and rubric can be found in Appendix C.

What separates the way Mrs. Westbrook used technology in her classroom circa 2014 from the way she used it in 2006? While her pedagogical stance has remained firmly grounded in critical thinking and high-level discourse, she believed that in 2014, her students were engaged in more authentic discourse that reflected not only their knowledge of the text but also their growing awareness of rhetoric and its connection to purpose and meaning. They were also more engaged because she was more mindful of using technology authentically so that the discourse of the technology she used matched the discourse of the classroom. That purposeful stance and the purposeful balancing of technology with deep content knowledge are key to integrating technology in a way that truly educates students.

Digital Learning Day

Digital learning should be the norm, not an isolated event that happens on one day a year. Back in 2012 the first national Digital Learning Day took place across the country. This initiative was the brainchild of the Alliance for Excellent Education, which is based on Washington, DC. The premise behind Digital Learning Day is to highlight the many innovative ways educators are consistently integrating technology to enhance and support student learning. Digital Learning Day has provided a powerful venue for education leaders to highlight great teaching practices and showcase innovative teachers, leaders, and instructional technology programs that are improving student outcomes. This grassroots effort blossomed into a massive, nationwide celebration as teachers realized that Digital Learning Day is not about technology but learning (Alliance for Excellent Education, 2014).

A digital learning culture was created at NMHS where teachers seized the opportunity to share uncommon learning activities that had become embedded across the curriculum. Below are some examples that I showcased during the inaugural Digital Learning Day in 2012:

- In Mrs. Collentine's humanities class, students worked in the computer lab on researching the history of drama and theater in the culture of their own heritage. They then had to create a Prezi (prezi.com), PowerPoint, or Google Doc presentation to be shared at a later time on what they found or learned to the class aligned to the Common Core State Standards.
- One of the biggest fears among students in an inquiry-based setting is that they don't feel ready for the discovery task. They also feel that the teacher is too smart, and just because she solved a problem easily on the board doesn't mean they will be able to do the same. Ms. Chowdhury's plan in physics had students use their mobile learning devices (smartphones, tablets, or laptops) to create screen casts of them solving a dynamics problem with details of every step. The students then kept the screen cast as live notes to use on any homework assignment or before a test. The advantage of solving the problem on screen cast versus notes is that it records their voices, so they can hear the reasoning behind doing a step the way it was done. She also planned to use these screen casts the following year to show students that other students, just like them, had solved the same problems before, so they can find comfort in knowing that nothing is being demanded of them that is beyond their ability.
- Mrs. Groff's digital journalism class researched and wrote stories, as per any other normal day in class. Her other English classes took virtual tours of the Globe

Theater and learned stage directions for the Shakespearean historical play, *Julius Caesar*.

- Mr. Fiscina's honors geometry students were instructed Tuesday in class that their homework was to log onto Edmodo (www.edmodo.com) and watch a lesson about the area of regular polygons. He used an app on his iPad called Educreations (www.educreations.com) to create the lesson. Students came into class on Digital Learning Day and were given an assignment that needed to be completed. Students who understood the lesson got started right away. Students who needed help were able to ask questions and get assistance from Mr. Fiscina. The class was then sectioned off for students in three categories (understood the lesson, only a few questions, and need a lot of help). This way Mr. Fiscina was able to spend the most time with the students who needed a great deal of help and less time with the students who understood the lesson. Challenge problems were given for students who mastered the material quickly. All work was collected and checked for understanding and conceptual mastery. He also had students use Poll Everywhere (www.polleverywhere.com) to check for understanding at the beginning of the lesson.

- Ms. Perna utilized computers with her classes to facilitate student learning and growth. Students in her US I classes conducted research to help them work on the writing process. Students in US I CP went through the research process to develop an outline for an essay focusing on which of the early presidents they believe was most effective and influential. Students in US I conducted research to write a biography on an influential early American. Her US II classes worked on a Roaring Twenties project. They put together, in a creative manner, a presentation on one cultural aspect of the 1920s (music, fashion, women, food, etc.) that would be presented in class at the end of the week during a Roaring Twenties Cultural Day.

IMPLEMENTATION TIPS

- Ensure infrastructure will support the initiative.
- Establish a shared vision and plan that outlines an expectation for digital learning.
- Support staff with relevant, applicable, and consistent professional learning.
- Monitor with the intent to ensure focus and sustainability.
- Replicate digital learning successes of other schools and districts.

SUMMARY

Uncommon learning results when educators effectively integrate digital tools with purpose to support or enhance student learning. Digital learning not only allows students to construct new knowledge, apply an array of skills that were just acquired, and demonstrate conceptual mastery in a variety of ways but also plays a huge role in building a sense of meaning and relevancy among learners. By allowing students the opportunity to choose which tools to allow them to best showcase what they know or can do empowers them to take ownership of their learning. Finding the natural pedagogical fit for technology in a digital environment, being able to assess learning in some form, and providing feedback to students are essential elements that all educators need to be cognizant of for digital learning to succeed.

Makerspaces

Culture does not change because we desire to change it. Culture changes when the organization is transformed— the culture reflects the realities of people working together every day.

—Frances Hesselbein

Societal changes are quickly beginning to impact the learning cultures of schools. One significant evolution is that of the Maker Movement. In simple terms this phenomenon represents a global community of inventors, designers, engineers, artists, programmers, hackers, tinkerers, craftspeople, and do-it-yourselfers (DIYers). These types of people see innovation and learning as a single element driven by curiosity. As they create or make things, they are constantly thinking about how it can be done differently the next time. The design cycle is all about reiteration, trying something again and again until it works, and then, once it works, making it better (Stewart, 2014).

As tools to make things continue to become better, cheaper, and more accessible, the Maker Movement is gaining momentum at rates that could never have been anticipated. This sweeping phenomenon has quickly found its way into a few schools across the globe where students and teachers alike have embraced the learning bounties inherent in the Maker Movement. The creative process of physically constructing an object is an effective way for students to both develop and demonstrate understanding (Papert, 1993). If the invitation to creativity is accompanied by intentional structure and guidance, maker activities can be channeled to support deep student learning (Blikstein, 2013; Vossoughi, Escudé, Kong, & Hooper, 2013).

THE BEGINNINGS OF A MAKERSPACE

During the period of transformation that spanned five years, the staff at New Milford High School (NHMS) had been diligently creating our own unique learning environments for our students. Building on the success of our bring your own device (BYOD) implementation, we had been hard at work to create an innovative learning space that would inspire and engage our students in new ways. With a school culture ripe for change and transformation, the missing piece was a 21st-century media specialist to take us to the next level.

When the position of library media specialist became available, Laura Fleming was the only person that I wanted for the position. She was hired with one major objective, and that was to transform the media center into a vibrant learning space. For years it was a place that students and staff alike avoided. Outdated books filled the stacks, food and drink were not allowed, student devices were prohibited, and senseless rules were consistently enforced. It needed a digital-age and pedagogical reboot. Without any specific guidance from me, I bestowed upon her autonomy over the budget and space that eventually laid the foundation for change. However, it was her unrelenting desire to create a space that worked for kids that led to a total transformation.

After coming on board she had done nothing less than blaze a trail. Ms. Fleming laid out her plans to create a makerspace, which resulted in one of the most amazing transformations that had taken place at NMHS in recent memory in what was our traditional library. A makerspace is a metaphor for a unique learning environment that encourages tinkering, play, and open-ended exploration for all (Fleming, personal communication, 2015a). I offered whatever assistance I could give in terms of monetary support and then did the next best thing I could do—*I got out of her way*. Never once did I second-guess what she was doing or purchasing as I knew when I hired her that she was a doer, difference maker, and spark plug for change. She embraced the autonomy she was given in a position that functioned as a librarian, media specialist, and educational technology integrator to push the envelope.

The learning space that was once in the traditional library has now been taken over by the students. Ms. Fleming knew that once the space was up and running, it would only continue to evolve. She then got out of the way of the students. By respecting their voices, she empowered them to take ownership of the makerspace. Thus the baton has been passed, and now the students are in charge. In the context of NMHS, a space that was once a barren wasteland was transformed into a thriving, learning metropolis where students flock to tinker, invent, create, collaborate, work, and most importantly, learn. When I hired Ms. Fleming, I basically told her the budget and that she had complete control of how she wanted to use the money. I could never have imagined how quickly she could radically transform this outdated space, using money that previously had always been spent on books, magazines, and electronic databases. Uncommon learning results when autonomy, trust, and support become the norm.

The Evolution of a Makerspace

How many times and in how many places have we seen it in recent years: school libraries and media centers the world

> Uncommon learning results when autonomy, trust, and support become the norm.

over unfrequented and underused? Even where they have been renovated, refurbished, and turned into state-of-the-art spaces, too often they remain desolate and dismal places. Faced with a library that hadn't been renovated in decades, Laura Fleming, the library media specialist at NMHS, knew from her experience that there was more to making her school library relevant than simply state-of-the-art facilities.

Charged with the task of remaking the library at NMHS, Ms. Fleming knew that the process of transformation for this forgotten space had to start with the culture that inhabited the space. She knew she was in a school that looked to the future, not to the past, one that sought to create an environment for staff and students alike that enabled collaboration, promoted innovation, and encouraged risk taking. Her goal from the outset therefore was to build a culture that would support the already rich and burgeoning environment that was growing within the school.

In researching practical strategies for cultivating a strong, creative culture, Ms. Fleming came across the Open University's (2013) "Innovating Pedagogy Report," which explored new forms of teaching, learning, and assessment and served as a guide, she felt, for educators and policy makers. Among the many innovations listed in this report was the notion of creating and nurturing a *maker culture* as a new idea (or at least a new working of a number of old ideas) and a new pedagogy that could transform education. Ms. Fleming had already experienced and absorbed some of the maker principles through her work with the transmedia story *Inanimate Alice* (www.inanimatealice.com) at a Mozilla Maker Party. Even from that brief introduction, she had seen that the affordances offered by digital technologies and new media allowed for enhanced opportunities to create a maker culture in schools like never before. A maker culture emphasizes informal, networked, peer-led, and shared learning motivated by fun and self-fulfillment (Open University, 2013). Ms. Fleming knew right away that this was what her library (and the school) were missing, and it was just what was needed to foster a whole new feeling in the school around the library, turning it into a vibrant, relevant part of the school community. She wanted teachers and students to actively want to visit the library and not simply find it an amenable space when they happened to be there.

This was the starting point for Ms. Fleming's attempt to radically shift the culture in the library and thereby add to the ongoing culture shift happening throughout the school. In designing a makerspace for the library, Ms. Fleming spoke at length with the students of NMHS about their creative interests and spent time just observing them on the computers and their devices at school. It was *their* reality she wanted *their*

The makerspace designed by Laura Fleming at New Milford High School

makerspace to reflect because whatever it became, it had to be something *they* wanted and found relevant. She also looked closely at the existing curricula at NMHS. Based on all of her findings, she developed a number of themes for her makerspace that filled in gaps in the school's offerings, that extended STEM-related concepts beyond the classroom walls, that made them accessible for all, and that also included some that were new and cutting edge to the entire school community.

What's in a Makerspace

After developing the themes for the space, Ms. Fleming then began stocking the space with materials to support each theme. The beauty of a makerspace is that there is no wrong way to outfit it with technologies and other items that allow students to tinker, invent, create, and make to learn. These included things such as the following:

- Legos—Architectural, Simple Machines
- Raspberry Pi (www.raspberrypi.org)
- 3-D Makerbot Printing Station (www.makerbot.com)
- Makey Makey Kits (makeymakey.com)
- littleBits (littlebits.cc)
- Arduino Boards (www.arduino.cc)
- Molecular Gastronomy Kits (www.molecule-r.com)
- Robot Kits
- Papertronics
- Wearable Technology Items

With the themes developed and the equipment procurement under way, it was time for Ms. Fleming to design the physical makerspace. To set up the physical space, she used her school's existing resources, including some library tables and bookshelves. Architecting the space was very much a collective effort and, having shared her plans with the school community, Ms. Fleming received great input from the school's tech team, the skills of the custodians, as well as an

enthusiastic bunch of students who were interested in "making" experiences and who were eager to see a place like this in their school and therefore wanted to contribute. By the end of this initial process, the physical makerspace ended up being a learning environment that encouraged creativity and ideas in designing and constructing a wide variety of 3-D artifacts.

The layout of the makerspace consists of *fixed* stations and *flexible* stations. The fixed stations are areas that are out in the makerspace all of the time for students to walk in, sit down at, and engage with. These include a littleBits Bar, where students have the opportunity to participate in using modular electronics to invent their own creations; a Take-Apart Tech Station (or *breaker space*), where computers are provided and designated for students specifically to disassemble, investigate, and build; a Lego table in which students can bring STEM concepts to life; a Makey Makey station, which allows students to turn any object into a game controller; and a 3-D design and printing station to bring their designs and ideas to life. For Ms. Fleming, the impetus to choose these as our fixed stations was simple; she wanted to include activities that students would be able to start and complete during their time-limited visits to the space as well as have them be able to do so independently, with little instruction needed. These informal learning pieces have been key in students wanting to visit the space and engage with the activities here during their free time. Also included in the design of the makerspace were some flexible stations. These include activities that rotate in and out of the space or are things that can be uplifted and taken to classrooms for collaboration with classroom teachers during more formalized instruction sessions. Some examples of this include molecular gastronomy, robotics, and electric circuitry.

One of the highlights of the makerspace at NMHS is their Smart TV. Each day, Ms. Fleming displays on the Smart TV something she calls a "digital bread crumb," a puzzle or a task or an activity designed to challenge and provoke. She uses these eye-catching displays and high-interest activities to draw students into the makerspace. Sometimes this might include playing a virtual musical instrument or playing a game of some kind. More often than not, students who have never visited the makerspace before are drawn in by this and, after engaging with our Smart TV, find themselves in the middle of the makerspace and exploring some of the other activities there.

The library at NMHS is open throughout the whole school day. With no scheduled classes, this means that all students have access to the space during their lunch periods, independent study, and collaborative lessons with classroom teachers at any time in the school day. As Sergey Brin, one of the founders of Google, has said, "Once you get too many rules, that will stifle innovation" (Carmody, 2012). Influenced

by this philosophy, everything in the NMHS Makerspace is hands-on, and nothing is off-limits (within the obvious bounds of safety).

Ms. Fleming also believes that every child has the right to invent, to tinker, to create, to innovate, and to make and do, and she believes in giving them the trust and flexibility to do so with only the lightest level of supervision compatible with ensuring a safe, busy, and industrious environment. This belief is what drove her mission to establish a makerspace at NMHS and one that has helped sustain it and enable it to flourish. Their makerspace transcends the usual constraints of academic potential, social barriers, and even language and development. Students of all levels can take full advantage of the resources and activities in this space and often take it upon themselves to help their peers and inspire them to experiment, make, and do. The makerspace sometimes is filled with engineering and conceptual physics students but also English language learners and special needs students. They truly have democratized the tools and skills necessary to design and make things that are of interest to our students while, at the same time, exposing them all to a new world of possibilities. Their makerspace is learner-driven and exploits the idea of experiential learning. It is a mash-up of differentiated learning experiences combining traditional elements and new technologies.

In designing learning experiences, we need to consider the technologies, resources, and materials around us and how they can be leveraged to engage and reach our learners. But even more important than all of these critical factors, the NMHS makerspace has been successful in encouraging meaningful student learning through the deliberate and enlightened cultivation of a culture of innovation in the school through play and open-ended exploration for all students.

THE MAKERSPACE IN ACTION

Ms. Fleming often hosts other teachers and their classes in this new space to offer uncommon learning experiences that compliment a variety of content areas. On one occasion she collaborated with Mr. Fowler and his conceptual physics classes for some hands-on experiences with electronics in the makerspace. Prior to their experience in this space, students had worked with the pHET DC Circuit Simulator (http://phet .colorado.edu/en/simulation/circuit-construction-kit-dc). They were able to explore current flows through lightbulbs in circuits powered by batteries and controlled by switches. This simulation experience gave the students some cause-and-effect experiences, allowing them to witness the interplay among voltage, current, and resistance. Despite these experiences, they missed the reality of low batteries, poor electrical connections, and other real-world experiences that impact circuits. This all changed dramatically when students were afforded a hands-on, authentic learning experience in the makerspace that allowed them to create artifacts of learning to demonstrate conceptual mastery.

Once in the makerspace, students began to create, tinker, and invent to learn concepts related to circuitry. When they made littleBits (http://littlebits.cc/) circuits that rotated paper hands and Snaptricity (http://www.snapcircuits.net/) circuits that launched propellers, they overcame initial impediments and experienced success. They had to troubleshoot to find a broken lead on a connection to the battery or find an open circuit because a connection that appeared to be made was electrically disconnected. The support provided by Ms. Fleming was excellent and pivotal to the success of the lesson. Kits were readily available for the students to use. When batteries ran low, she had backups on hand for all of the groups. Two students gravitated more toward the Legos, and she immediately improvised by having electronic motors available that they could work with. This experience has provided a reservoir of learning opportunities for both of

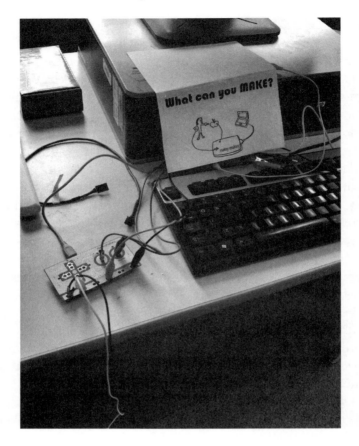

Mr. Fowler's classes that they continue to draw from when working through series and parallel circuits.

While studying the unit on visual merchandising and display marketing, Mrs. Vicari thought about our school store, which was currently being redesigned and reopened. She then challenged the students to use all the elements of visual merchandising and display to create a model of what our school store should look like. Their project was to design the school store's storefront, sign, entrance, window display, selling space, storage space, personnel space, customer space, color, lighting, graphics, paint, fixtures, point-of-purchase display, and props. Collaborating with Ms. Fleming, who introduced Mrs. Vicari to Tinkercad (https://tinkercad.com/), she challenged the students to use this Web site to create a 3-D model of their school store, which could be printed out in plastic using the Makerbot 3-D printer that was a main component of our makerspace. The students also elaborated on their design with a written explanation that included all the elements of visual merchandising.

The makerspace in the library is an oasis for student self-directed learning. It serves as a rejuvenation center for inspiring love for both formal and informal learning. In my opinion, a space like this should be a priority for all schools in the 21st century, and you do not have to break the bank to create one. "This idea of making has really sparked a revolution in learning and there are opportunities for all educators to create unique learning environments that best serve our 21st-century learners" (Fleming, 2015a).

ESSENTIAL QUALITIES OF A MAKERSPACE

Educators can easily and quickly integrate a makerspace into the learning experience at their respective schools. The key though is not to decide haphazardly on a whim to create this authentic, inquiry-based learning initiative but to thoughtfully plan everything out prior to implementation. Just like any other new initiative, success depends on proper planning, support, and a process to ensure sustainability. A makerspace can pose a fearful initiative to many teachers and administrators alike as a certain amount of control has to be given up. Additionally students need to be trusted as they will be operating in this space quite often with little or no supervision.

When beginning to explore the implementation of a makerspace, it is important to consider these three crucial elements: process, dedicated educator, and space. As with any process, making requires the ability for educators to give up control and trust students. It can be messy and unpredictable, but the products students create, problems they solve, and questions they answer become relevant learning experiences they value.

The process of making requires a simple vision where students are empowered to create an artifact through self-directed learning. In the space they are guided by natural inquiry and an innate desire to explore interests by doing. This requires two specific skill sets that develop the space into a catalyst of creativity through the process of making to learn. The first skill set is knowing which tool to use and how to use it safely. Students in a makerspace will have access to an array of tools, some of which they are familiar with, while others they might have never used or seen before. For the most part it will be up to them to figure out and determine the right tools for the right job while being provided guidance from a teacher on safe and responsible use. Avoid the common pitfall of equating making with just the tools. Although high-powered tools can be seductive, remember that making is a creative, person-led process. Making can include students lying on pillows on the floor crocheting or sitting at tables with cardboard and glue. A room filled with tools but missing makers and their work is like an empty computer lab (Bevan, Petrich, & Wilkinson, 2014). The second skill set is a combination of problem solving and diagnostic skills required to figure out why something won't work while coming up with a creative solution without getting frustrated. Not only are these skills essential to success in K–12 learning but also the real world.

The second key element that must be considered when developing a makerspace is the selection of the right educator who will oversee the initiative. The process of making requires patience on behalf of an educator who will not have all the answers nor know how to help students out every time they experience a problem. This is quite OK as it is near impossible for someone to have all of the required content knowledge to assist students as they make to learn. This special person assists students to diagnose a problem so that they can create a solution while guiding them through the inevitable highs and lows of making something. He or she does not have to be an expert in engineering, technology, mathematics, or other niche content area.

What he or she must possess is basic knowledge on the fundamental characteristics of makerspaces including items to purchase, inquiry-based learning, self-directed learning, and most importantly a passion for guiding students during the making process. This type of educator ties making to different content areas and has demonstrated a shift in his or her professional practice from transmitting knowledge to enabling a student to create his or her own solution. The best way to describe the style needed for a makerspace to be successful is that of a coach who models when necessary. Laura Fleming is that type of dedicated educator.

> Teacher librarians can also act as a cross-disciplinary resource that can glue many of the curricular areas together by offering great informal learning to supplement the formal curriculum. I have done this through the creation of my makerspace. Through this space, we have democratized STEM-related concepts, making them accessible to the entire school community, all throughout the school day. Libraries have long offered opportunities for collaboration, communication, and community-based learning. I think we have a responsibility as teacher librarians to provide opportunities like this for our students. (Fleming, 2015a)

Without her and the defining characteristics she possessed, the success of the makerspace she oversaw would probably never have materialized. Figure 4.1, created by Dr. Jackie Gerstein (2014), identifies important characteristics that a maker educator should possess.

The final essential quality is the space itself. This can be a challenge as available areas to set up a makerspace in many schools are few and far between. The perfect space must encourage creativity and support the idea that anything is possible. It should contain comfortable seating, have limited rules and control, be flexible, have ubiquitous access to Wi-Fi and technology, and infuse prompts and guides to promote

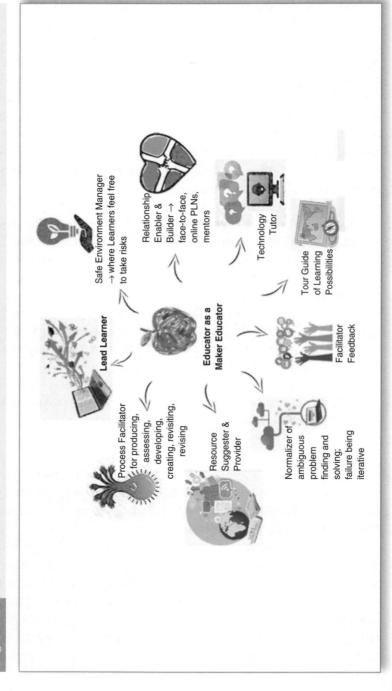

Figure 4.1

Safe Environment Manager → where Learners feel free to take risks

Relationship Enabler & Builder → face-to-face, online PLNs, mentors

Lead Learner

Technology Tutor

Tour Guide of Learning Possibilities

Educator as a Maker Educator

Facilitator Feedback

Process Facilitator for producing, assessing, developing, creating, revisiting, revising

Resource Suggester & Provider

Normalizer of ambiguous problem finding and solving; failure being iterative inquiry. For the selected space to be successful, it should be accessible for students at all times during the day, not just dedicated class time. Typical areas where makerspaces flourish include school libraries or media centers, specific classrooms that focus on the arts and sciences, or other common areas that are underutilized in a building. You can even develop a pop-up makerspace or a makerspace on a cart. The possibilities are limited only to your imagination.

Dedicated makerspaces can promote a new level of commitment to making; projects can be left out overnight, and specialized tools can be sectioned off (Bevan et al., 2014). The success of the makerspace at NMHS rested on the fact that the media center was accessible all day, an array of tools and materials were provided, and students were trusted to direct their own learning with limited supervision. The possible locations to design a makerspace are by no means a definitive list. Obviously a space is needed to create a makerspace, but any educator can cultivate a maker mind-set in his or her classroom. All it takes is the willingness to let students tinker, create, invent, and make to learn while providing them with the tools to do so. For more information on integrating the concept of making to learn in your classroom or school, visit the Maker Education Initiative (http://www.makered.org). Appendix D provides a rubric developed by Lisa Yokana (2015) that can be used to assess skills and behaviors associated with learning in a maker environment. Additional information is provided in Appendix E to assist you with developing your own unique makerspace.

IMPACT OF A MAKERSPACE

Alan is a freshman at a high school in Baltimore. He has always had an interest in computers, but that increased even more thanks to the library makerspace at his school. When he started school in the fall of 2014, he found out that the makerspace had a take-apart tech station where students could visit and take apart computers. Through this he learned the parts of a computer. He enjoyed the experience so much that he and his friends decided to challenge themselves and began to think what they could do with computers. They decided to not only take a computer apart but also to put it back together. In time they also decided to make a new computer case to put the computers they built in.

The first thing they had to do was find a working computer to take apart. Once they did that, Alan and his friends carefully took everything out of it. There were a lot of screws and parts to disassemble. It took them about three days of working on it to get everything out without breaking any of the parts. After the computer was completely taken apart, they then began to think of ideas for making a new computer case. The group started looking around the library and in the back room until they spotted saw some empty boxes. This is when they decided to turn a regular cardboard box into their new computer case!

Alan and company planned out how they would arrange the computer components in the box and drew lines where they wanted all of the parts to be. Instead of screws, a hot glue gun was used to attach the pieces to where the students wanted them to be in the box. They cut out pieces of the box to make cutouts for all of the plugs. To do this, Alan measured the pieces and the sizes of the holes that needed to be cut in the box. After that they only had to put the hard drive and the CD drive into the new case, and on day four a new computer was assembled.

At that point Alan and his friends attached a monitor and a power supply and turned the new computer on to test it. As amateur technicians, the students were not surprised when they encountered a few problems. The students then spent some time researching the error messages that they were receiving. After a few hours, and with the help of Mr. Sepulveda, a member of the school information technology (IT) department, the students figured out the adjustments that they needed to make. After successfully booting up the new computer, Mr. Sepulveda created a user account for them to be able to login and gain full access to the device they made. The group then set it up so that other people in the library could use and test it out too. Right away students were logging on and using the computer to play games and do their work. They were shocked that a computer in a cardboard box could work. After a few days, Alan and his friends moved their computer out into the showcase of the school's hallway.

If it weren't for a committed librarian and IT specialist, none of this would have been possible for Alan and his friends. Thanks to the support and commitment of these innovative educators, a makerspace provided students with an authentic learning experience like no other. Although this project was difficult at times, Alan and his friends found it to be fun, and they were proud to have pulled it off. A few days later, they wanted to try the same thing again and this time decided to turn an old G5 Mac into a Windows-based PC. This is learning at its best.

At this point the group decided to create a Web site to share their creations with other schools around the world. Their hope was that students and teachers all over will learn from and be inspired by their work. Not only did they hope others would learn from it, but Alan hoped they would participate in it as well. Visitors can register on their site to receive updates, post messages and questions in the forum, and participate in regular challenges. One such challenge for other students was to build their own computers and put them in creative cases. Students who do this can submit creations to Alan's group, and they will post them in the picture gallery on the site. The students were proud of the fact that they received comments from teachers all over the country on their site. Alan in particular was proud that a student contacted him to tell him how much the Web site impacted her and a project she was working on. He was even contacted by a librarian looking for his help in setting up a makerspace for her library! Alan knows that this is just the beginning for them, and they have plans to continue taking apart computers, creating creative computer cases, and sharing them on their site. Their hope is to inspire other makers to do the same.

IMPLEMENTATION TIPS

- Identify a dedicated educator.
- Secure a space.
- Systematically plan (Fleming, 2015b).
  - Understand your learners.
  - Assess existing curricula, programs, and offerings within the school community.
  - Consider global trends and best practices.
  - Develop themes.
  - Order equipment and materials.
- Establish an environment that trusts students.

SUMMARY

The Maker Movement has resulted in an infinite amount of uncommon learning pathways for today's students. By embracing a DIY mentality, students can engage in inquiry-based, self-directed activities where a true ownership of learning is actively embraced. Makerspaces provide a cost-effective approach that schools can employ to allow students to follow their passions by tinkering, inventing, creating, and making to learn. The story of Laura Fleming's maker-space initiative illustrates the endless and innovative learning possibilities that students can engage in, which directly and indirectly support the curriculum and interdisciplinary connections. When beginning to think about implementing your own makerspace, thoroughly plan out the initiative focusing on establishing a vision for the making process, purchasing necessary tools, identifying the right educator to serve as facilitator, and select the perfect space. Once the makerspace is up and running, it will begin to run itself as the students themselves will eventually dictate the type of learning activities and projects they want to engage in. In the end this will bring about a greater sense of relevancy and meaning among students in terms of their learning at school. In the words of Laura Fleming (2015b), "If you let them build it, they will learn."

Blended and
Virtual Learning

ace-to-face schooling no longer meets the diverse
learning needs of all students. This chapter will address
how schools can easily implement both blended and virtual
learning opportunities to personalize and individualize
instruction with technology. Blended learning is a component
of a student's formal K–12 education. The Clayton Christensen Institute (2012) breaks down the definition of blended
learning into three components:

1. In part through online learning, with some element of
   student control over time, place, path, and/or pace;

2. In part in a supervised physical location away from
   home; and

3. The modalities along each student's learning path
   within a course or subject are connected to provide an
   integrated learning experience

The maximization of learning time is amplified as more educators and schools move to totally virtual learning experiences where students direct their own learning by exploring their interests and passions in more detail. In an extensive study, the U.S. Department of Education found that students in online conditions performed modestly better, on average, than those learning the same material through traditional face-to-face instruction (2010, p. xiv). What was even more significant was that when instruction combined online and face-to-face elements, there was a larger advantage relative to purely face-to-face instruction than with purely online instruction (p. xv).

The technology tools inherent in both virtual and blended learning models offer additional advantages as well. For example, data analytics can identify students who need early intervention, thus increasing retention. Another added benefit is the student performance analytics, which can be used to study and better understand student learning. The online tools available in blended courses can also significantly enhance student engagement, ensuring that all students participate in course discussions and benefit from collaborative learning (U.S. Department of Education, 2010). The Mooresville Graded School District has seen an improvement of 20 percentage points—from 68 to 88 percent—in the portion of its students who scored "proficient" on all core-subject state exams in the subjects of reading, math, and science in the four years since its conversion to a one-to-one laptop program in support of blended learning initiatives (Vander Ark, 2014).

This chapter will discuss both pathways as uncommon learning initiatives to individualize and personalize both the school and learning experience for students.

A BLENDED SCHOOL EXPERIENCE

At the Mandell School in New York City, students experience a seamless integration of digital and physical learning spaces. Teachers transition classes between online and face-to-face discussions and activities much in the same way a class may transition from one subject to the next. A window into one class would likely show clusters of students working at various paces through digitally delivered content or collaborating via a shared platform, while the teacher works alongside individual students or small groups to aid in task comprehension. In the room next door, the class may be Skyping with a class from France as part of a language exchange then collaborating on a shared document to swap cultural experiences. Morning announcements stream live through Google video calls to homerooms, with anchors passing the mic to go "on location" to different classes for special announcements.

At Mandell, the term *blended learning* is used infrequently, more often replaced with simply *learning*. When school leaders designed the academic program, they did so with three mission-based goals in mind: personalization, collaboration, and activism. Creating a blended environment was not among the shared values but rather a pathway to achieving these values.

Blending to Personalize

The differentiation of instruction presents a challenge for educators wary of creating visible separation by leveled grouping within a class. Moreover, physical groupings tend to be inflexible once formed and, thus, far from ideal in meeting the dynamic needs of students. Mandell was committed to providing individualized paths within heterogeneous groups. School leaders believed the key to fulfilling this commitment would be found by combining teacher expertise in differentiation and deep knowledge of students with powerful technology tools that could adapt to learner needs. To help teachers create divergent paths within a single instructional environment, Mandell implemented a rotation model of blended learning, whereby students transition into and out of online content delivery and practice.

Over time, the personalization of learning through a blended model grew to include several constructs.

- **Daily Sequence:** For math students, daily plans and activities are delivered through a shared document in Google Drive. Teachers build the plans to represent unique learning needs within each group with whom the document is shared. Support resources, including video lessons and practice links, are included in the sequence. The delivery of the document via a digital path allows for private, dispersed, and flexible grouping day to day.
- **WRM Lab:** To develop skills mastery on an individual level for writing, reading, and math, the Mandell School created a lab period once a rotation during which students received a personalized lesson based on formative assessment and student data. During this block, there are teams of teachers to assist students as they flow from instruction to practice. Instruction is often delivered via multimedia or online resource, but it is sometimes delivered by the teacher to meet the unique style of learners. The practice component of the exercise combines online interaction with offline documentation.
- **Project-Based Learning:** A tool frequently used to pique interest and solicit project ideas from students is the survey form. Forms generate data on student interests and preferred learning modes, data teachers then use to construct projects that very often involve creative technologies and coding.
- **Adaptive Software:** The use of programs like Khan Academy (www.khanacademy.org), EPGY-Redbird (epgy.stanford.edu), Duolingo, and Moby Max, among others, provide teachers with data points to measure student mastery. Additionally, with input from teachers, the sequence of practice can bend and expand to meet learner needs.
- **Flipped Instruction:** A balanced approach to flipped instruction, where the model is implemented as one of many within a class, creates opportunity for guided practice in school following content delivery outside of class via digital content.

Blending to Collaborate

To Mandell leaders, the personalization of the learning environments also meant opening more paths through which students could connect with their teachers and each other. By blending features of the digital platforms such as chat, discussion boards, and e-mail with face-to-face communication, teachers could meet students where they felt most comfortable expressing their voices.

One of the first initiatives addressing this targeted outcome was the summer reading discussions conducted through a group within Schoology (www.schoology.com), a learning management software (LMS) the school chose to create digital classroom and group spaces. Students and teachers used the space to share perspectives on the summer reading selections and share titles they had selected for independent reading. Aside from teaching students how to use social space for academic discussions, teachers hoped to build relationships between new students and the community. Tiffany Della Vedova, head of Upper School, spoke to the success of the initiative:

> We were surprised by the depth of friendship formed. The first summer, two new students realized they were both in Morocco posting about their reading. They quickly connected and became friends even before meeting face-to-face. Each year, teachers have witnessed friendships begin in this online space, augmenting the anticipation for the start of school and bringing a new level of excitement to the first interaction. (Della Vedova, personal communication, 2014)

The summer learning group now remains an open share space during the school year, and students continue to share their love of reading and learning within the space. The creation of this digital share space has done far more than engender peer relationships as teachers have also come to witness the intrinsic motivation of social connection in learning.

The emphasis on collaboration as an essential 21st-century skill has grown as the world has become connected in more complex ways through technology. Mandell leaders recognized the skill set required to work together in digital spaces was one that needed to be taught, modeled, and practiced in action. A blended learning environment would create a sandbox approach to teaching the type of collaboration taking place within large, global organizations and businesses. At first, teachers used collaborative tools such as Google Apps for Education and Prezi to form project partnerships within the school. As the program grew, these partnerships extended beyond the school walls into the digital realm. The following projects are examples of this type of networked collaboration:

- In global history, students participate in the Global Students–Global Perspectives, 5 Most Pressing Problems of the Planet Project. Project creators, Laurie Clement, an elementary school teacher in Windsor, Ontario Canada, and Mark Engstrom, a MS assistant principal and eighth-grade geography teacher at the Graded School in São Paulo, Brazil, designed the project as "an international collaboration of middle school students around the concept of global issues," according to the Global Students–Global Perspectives Web site, which can be accessed at sites.google.com/a/mytools2go.ca/ globalstudentsglobalperspectives/home.
- In technology class, students learn how to use basic coding to build a Web site on a topic of their choice. During this process, they work with a mentor matched to their expertise. Project mentors reside in multiple locations throughout the city and country, and students use communication technology to connect with their mentors, learning about digital communication standards at a professional level.
- Through the use of ePals in language, students develop pen-pal relationships while engaged in a language exchange. The relationships have continued as students matriculate through grade levels. In 2013 and 2014, students were able to bring their digital

connection to the face-to-face environment when Mandell welcomed a visiting class from Perpignan, France, with whom students had been collaborating for two years via ePals. French teacher Sherman Caldwell recalls this special project culmination:

> I can think of no better way to bring a language to life. The students quickly discovered that they were able to communicate with their new friends in French. They also discovered that they shared very similar interests even though their lifestyles were quite different. This collaboration was easily the most fascinating aspect of our course. (Della Vedova, 2014)

- In the global activism class, students connect to other classes through a Twitter chat, discussing global issues, sharing resources, and designing solutions. Students also use social media to promote service projects and school events.

Blending to Build Perspective

The Mandell School's focus on service learning as a cornerstone of the program was the third impetus for the design of a connected community. It was important for students to understand their roles as active citizens of not only their community but their planet. To develop empathy and design effective solutions to global issues, students have to explore them from different perspectives.

> Empathy grows authentically when relationships grow, and through these relationships, students are offered a window into another's experience. This was especially true as students tried to agree on the most pressing global problems within their globally diverse project groups. It quickly became clear that the most important issue in one area of the world might be just another headline in another. I recall one student sharing what she had learned about the daily fear of

violence faced by an Israeli group member who lived near Gaza. This is perspective-changing interaction we are seeking and finding through these global peer connections. (Della Vedova, 2014)

Like all teachers, the Mandell faculty strives to help students understand their world and come to recognize their responsibilities to it. However, they also sought to redefine the concept of *world* itself. The communities within the online world and the accompanying responsibilities remain nebulous for the greater global community; they are constantly changing with the rapid pace of innovation. Understanding digital responsibility is especially confusing for children who are growing in their understandings of world and self. Where it may not be possible to define the mores of a space ungoverned by a single shared culture, teachers at Mandell believed the onus rested with them to help students establish and practice a set of digital citizenship principles. "Posted on the door to my classroom is a digital citizenship contract created by and signed by my students and myself. Allowing students to create this contract provides them with a sense of ownership and responsibility regarding their behaviors and interactions within our online community. With the contract being posted at the entrance of our classroom, students have a daily reminder of the commitment they have made to themselves and to the other members within our digital community," says Michelle Cristella, middle school history (Della Vedova, 2014).

In implementing any programmatic component, a school must rely on its mission as its compass. For the Mandell School, the priorities of personalization, collaboration, and activism informed the structure and purpose of the program. Where these timeless tenets continue to guide program growth, new technologies are assessed using the SAMR model, with the target set on the *m*odification and *r*edefinition half of the framework. "For us, it has always been about bringing students closer to us, to each other, and to their learning. A blended learning environment has been essential to helping us actualize this goal at a transformational standard" (Della Vedova, 2014).

Blended Learning Models

There are many ways to successfully implement blended learning into a school or classroom. For the most part there are four main models: rotation, flex, à la carte, and enriched virtual. The rotation model is the most common model implemented in schools and can be adapted in a variety of ways, including the flipped classroom. The Clayton Christensen Institute (2012) outlines the main blended learning models concisely:

1. **Rotation Model.** In this model students rotate on a fixed schedule or at the teacher's discretion among learning modalities in a particular course or subject area. At least one of the rotations contains an online learning component. Other modalities that students might rotate through include small-group or full-class instruction, cooperative learning projects, independent study, individual tutoring, and traditional activities. The majority of learning happens in the physical school building, with the exception of homework assignments and extended projects. The District of Columbia Public Schools created a rotation model in 2012. For literacy, the stations include small groups, guided reading with an aide, vocabulary with a teacher, and independent online course work. Students use Lexia for foundational reading skills, and access digital books through myON reader. They also use the software programs ST Math and First in Math, which feature game-based instruction (DeNisco, 2014). There are several sub models of the rotation model, which include the following:

- *Station Rotation.* This model differs from the individual rotation model as students are directed to rotate through all of the stations, not only those on their custom schedules.
- *Lab Rotation.* Students rotate to a computer lab for the online learning station. This provides educators with the opportunity for targeted pullout and intervention services.

- *Flipped Classroom.* Students participate in online learning offsite in place of traditional homework and then attend the physical school for face-to-face, teacher-guided, and facilitated learning. The majority of the content and instruction is delivered online.
- *Individual Rotation.* Each student has an individualized playlist and does not necessarily rotate to each available station or modality. A teacher establishes each individual student schedule, or this is generated at random.

2. **Flex Model.** In this model, online activities become the foundation of student learning, even if students are directed to offline activities on occasion. Each student moves on a customized, fluid schedule among learning modalities. The classroom teacher is still present in the room, with the majority of student learning taking place at the school. The exception to this would be any homework assignments or projects assigned outside the school day. What makes this model powerful is that the teacher or other educators can provide face-to-face support on a flexible, adaptive, as-needed basis using a combination of small-group instruction, group projects, and individual tutoring. These schools are often set up like offices, with students in their own workspaces and a number of teachers circulating to provide support, while students complete online course work (DeNisco, 2014). Lewis and Clark High School, part of Vancouver Public Schools in Washington has two large *flex* areas where students do online instruction at permanently assigned workstations that are similar to office cubicles. There are five classrooms of different sizes that teachers can use when needed for group lessons and smaller spaces for projects or tutoring. The typical day varies from student to student and week to week, but often about half the time is spent on the computer with Edgenuity courses (http:// www.edgenuity.com) in every subject. The other half is spent working with teachers in individual tutoring or small-group instruction or with other students on group projects (DeNisco, 2014). Flex models may have face-to-face certified teachers

who supplement the online learning on a daily basis, whereas others may provide little face-to-face enrichment.

3. À La Carte Model. In this model a student takes a course entirely online to accompany other experiences that are available at a brick-and-mortar school or learning center. The teacher of record for the à la carte course is the online teacher. Students may take an à la carte course either at the school or offsite. This differs from full-time online learning because it is not a whole-school experience. A great example of this is the Independent OpenCourseWare Study (IOCS). The IOCS Program, developed by Tenafly Middle School teacher Juliana Meehan and myself as the New Milford High School (NMHS) principal and pioneered at NMHS, New Jersey, represents a bold, authentic learning experience for secondary students that allows them to fully utilize OpenCourseWare (OCW) to pursue learning that focuses on their passions, interests, and career aspirations. OCW can best be defined as high-quality digital publications created by leading American universities that are organized as courses of study, offered free of charge, and delivered via the Internet. OCW courses are available under open licenses, such as Creative Commons. These courses allow for personalization of studies as students explore topics of their choosing. IOCS is aligned to Common Core, International Society for Technology in Education (ISTE) NETS•S, and state technology curriculum standards as well as the Partnership for 21st Century Skills Framework for 21st Century Skills. IOCS students choose from an array of OCW offerings from schools such as the Massachusetts Institute of Technology (MIT), Harvard, Yale, University of California at Berkeley, Stanford, and many others and apply their learning to earn high school credit (Sheninger, 2014). A concise description of IOCS and aligned rubrics can be accessed at sites.google.com/site/opencoursewarestudies.

4. Enriched Virtual Model. With this model students have required face-to-face learning sessions with their teachers of record and then are free to complete their remaining course work remotely. Learning online becomes the essential learning

component when the students are located remotely. The same teacher typically serves as both the online and face-to-face teacher. This model varies from the flipped approach as students seldom meet face-to-face with their teachers every weekday. What differentiates the enriched virtual model from a fully online course is that face-to-face learning sessions are more than optional office hours or social events because they are required. The Rio Rancho Cyber Academy in New Mexico has students in Grades 6 through 8 come to school Monday, Wednesday, and Friday morning, while Grades 9 through 11 come in Tuesday and Thursday. Seniors come in only on Tuesdays. Students spend the other days at home working on online courses developed by Edgenuity. When students are in the school, instruction is focused on the concepts with which they are struggling. The school's eight teachers can work with students individually or in small groups (DeNisco, 2014).

For additional support check out the iNACOL Blended Learning Teacher Competency Framework at http://www .inacol.org/wp-content/uploads/2014/10/iNACOL-Blended-Learning-Teacher-Competency-Framework.pdf.

THE FLIPPED CLASSROOM

One of the most popular blended learning techniques is the flipped classroom. In 2007, John Bergmann and Aaron Sams, two high school chemistry teachers from Colorado, shifted their teaching practice dramatically. Where previously they had lectured to students during class time, they assigned their students homework tasks meant to reinforce the lecture, they flipped that model around. They created videos of their lectures and asked their students to watch them as homework then used in-class time to complete the tasks that used to be done at home. In-class time could now focus on experiments, discussions, and more active forms of learning. Students who did not watch the video had to watch it in class, while the rest did the activity and got help on the assignment that was taught in the video.

Over time, they began calling this the *flipped classroom* model of instruction, and it has spread rapidly (in various forms) to a large number of classrooms. There are two main components associated with the flipped classroom approach to teaching and learning. The first is that students watch lectures and consume other forms of content outside of school at their own pace while communicating with peers and teachers using online tools. The second is that students in school work to apply actively what they have learned through concept engagement with assistance from the teacher. While in school students can now use class time to absorb the material through problem solving and skill development (Ojalvo & Doyne 2011). Rycik (2012) found that teachers who flipped their classrooms reported using the extra class time to give valuable one-on-one assistance to students. The flipped classroom provides avenues for teachers to become facilitators of learning and move away from the sage-on-the-stage approach to teaching. The goal is to extend learning time conversation to outside of class through threaded discussion.

During this same time span, 1:1 classrooms—where each student has a computing device available to be used whenever needed—have also spread quickly. Even more popular than 1:1 school environments has been the implementation of bring your own device (BYOD) initiatives. This cost-effective strategy supplements student-owned technology with that which the school already owns to increase equitable access. As technology continues to get more powerful, more ubiquitous, and cheaper in the coming years, this trend is assured to continue. There is a huge opportunity for these two trends to join forces: that the principles of the flipped classroom model of instruction combined with the power of 1:1 or BYOD technology can create a *truly* flipped classroom where it isn't just the lectures and homework assignments that have been flipped but rather the underlying structure of the class itself. Here are three key areas in which such a shift can and should occur.

1. A Shift in Pacing

The vast majority of classrooms, especially at the secondary level, expect all students within a class to learn the given material in one set, standard amount of time. Combined with the power of the flipped classroom, 1:1 technology frees us to allow students to complete material at a more individualized pace. With students able to learn content through videos that can be watched and re-watched as needed, then work with that content at their own pace through online practice problems, simulations, or discussions, there's no need for us to force students through material in lockstep fashion. Individual classrooms can make major strides in individualizing student pacing on their own, but the real shift will come when entire schools choose to use mastery rather than seat time as the key indicator for when a student has completed a class.

2. A Shift in Classroom Ownership

Flipping the classroom can also lead to a fundamental shift in terms of who "owns" the class. Whereas the traditional classroom has been very teacher centered, the use of 1:1 technology allows for a much more student-centered classroom. Instead of students listening to a standard lecture, class time can now focus on specific student questions and wonderings, and the plan for any given day can adjust immediately based on student errors or misconceptions (as shown through real-time, online assessment data). A truly flipped classroom must shift to meet the needs of the students it serves.

3. A Shift From Passive Content Consumption to Active Content Creation

The traditional model of learning is one in which the students are generally passive recipients of content (such as a lecture). Even in the standard flipped classroom, the students remain passive during the homework time (when they watch videos) but are at least freed to be more active learners during class time. Happily, 1:1 technology can take this one step further: students can not only become active learners, but they can utilize the power of technology to create their own content for classmates and other learners throughout the world. Whether through a podcast, individual blog, classroom wiki, or another Web 2.0 tool, students can become the authors, lecturers, and collaborators working together to teach content to each other and to interested observers outside the classroom.

Flipping in Math

During the initial stages of Ms. Chellani's teaching career, she had dedicated a good portion of class time to lecture similar to the educator norms she had observed. Although she was teaching her students the content and the performance results were relatively decent overall, Ms. Chellani continually found herself limited in class time to provide her students with opportunities to develop higher-order thinking skills as well as the interactive experiences needed to keep her students engaged and motivated. She acknowledged the fact that she had to change her instructional practices at NMHS to make the learning experience more relevant, personalized, and engaging to her students. Through research, attending workshops and conferences, and discussions with her colleagues, she realized that the road that needed to be taken to achieve this goal was to flip instruction.

Although teaching students the content is very important, providing students with opportunities to dive deeper into mathematical concepts, promote higher-order thinking skills; make the learning experience more relevant to students by infusing technology into daily lessons; develop the skills needed to succeed in college, life, and the workplace; and apply the material to real-world instances to enhance comprehension and significance of the material taught are just as important, if not more. These are some of the key reasons flipping the classroom by assigning digital content as homework is beneficial; it provides educators with the gift of time to present these opportunities to students. Take a look at the following vignette to understand the effects of incorporating this curriculum tool into the learning process.

> Prior to the day's calculus class, Ms. Chellani had sent a video on position, velocity, and acceleration through her selected social networking platform, in this case, Edmodo, for the students to view as homework. Once they had viewed the material, they were prompted to answer five polls to ensure understanding of the material. Student results were submitted via the social networking platform. Ms. Chellani had access to the student results on her end and viewed them before the start of class to gage their level of comprehension. After students entered Ms. Chellani's classroom, they sat in their seats, took out their smartphones, and texted their answers to the warm-up question, based on the instructional video content assigned and displayed on the SMART board via an online polling tool. Once all students had submitted their responses, the results of the warm-up were revealed by Ms. Chellani. According to the results, approximately 70 percent of the class seemed to grasp the material, which correlated with the student results from the five polls. Ms. Chellani found this to be a teachable moment and fostered a discussion among the class by asking a series of questions on the content. She then revealed the results of the polls from the prior night on the SMART board. Students who answered the polls with incorrect responses realized their misconceptions. Ms. Chellani then proceeded with the day's lesson by placing students in collaborative pairs and having them engage in a case study on the relevant content for the remainder and majority of class. (Chellani, personal communication, 2015)

In addition to the vignette describing how flipping instruction and assigning digital content encourages collaboration and provides the luxury of time for the educator,

Ms. Chellani has seen students significantly benefit from viewing these learning resources prior to class. To start, as opposed to waiting for all students to be on the same page with the lecture, material, and writing the notes, they work at their own pace because they have the ability to pause, rewind, and fast-forward. As per the vignette, they come into class with a working knowledge of the topic, so questions on the material can be asked to facilitate a group discussion and to have more time to reinforce the learning through a variety of means (i.e., problem sets, collaborative assignments, case studies, etc.). Many of her students play sports after school, so to have homework assignments that they know will take a reasonable amount of time reduces their frustration with the material and ultimately improves their interest in the topic and the subject. Additionally, as students of varying levels are typically in a classroom, she has found digital content to be an effective way to personalize and differentiate the learning experience for her students.

For example, she had two special needs students in her algebra class who were not interested at all in math in general. She knew her challenge here was to make math more entertaining for them. She also knew she had the tools at her disposal to accomplish this goal. Her thought was to make it more fun and engaging for them by not only assigning a video or interactive tutorial but also an online math game for them to play on that same topic. She rolled it out to them to observe the results. Because the learning experience was personalized and catered to meet their needs, their enjoyment with math had improved. In fact, because they were more inclined to complete the interactive online game successfully, she noticed that their performance in class and on assessments had gradually improved as well. Thus, as you can see, assigning digital content has many advantages for not only the educator but for the student as well.

Although Ms. Chellani's classroom is currently flipped, the transition she made from traditional modes of teaching to creating a student-centered learning environment was gradual.

She did not want to overwhelm her students by drastically changing the instructional norms to which they were acclimated. To deviate from the largely lecture-based classroom, Ms. Chellani first incorporated a variety of tools into her daily lessons to differentiate the learning experience and infuse more technology before assigning digital content as homework. For example, instead of writing a warm-up question on the board at the beginning of class for students to answer with a show of hands, she decided to use an online polling tool with which students could answer the question anonymously by texting their results via their smartphones. When her students became used to the new format of the warm-up, she decided to make other changes such as infusing online review games and videos into her daily lessons to help supplement her instruction. Ms. Chellani found this highly advantageous as it exposed her students to a variety of online, instructional resources to help teach the content.

Once Ms. Chellani found her students to be receptive to the changes she had made in her classroom, she progressed toward flipping the classroom completely. She started assigning digital content as homework for students to view prior to coming to class via her selected learning management system. Ms. Chellani's practices transitioned to a more student-centered approach because she had her students drive the discussion and day's lesson on the material they had viewed as opposed to her. Because less and less time was spent on lecture as the days passed, there were more opportunities, interactive experiences, and assignments that were able to be presented to her students. Overtime, when Ms. Chellani's students learned that the traditional lectures on the content were not going to take place in class and that the foundational material was needed to engage successfully in collaborative exercises and hands-on opportunities to reinforce the learning, more and more students began to view the digital content. Eventually, nearly everyone was on board with the new instructional approach.

There is emerging research that supports the use of this blended learning approach. Marlowe (2012) found that lower-performing students showed the greatest increase in grades in a flipped classroom. Teachers found that there were more opportunities for small-group work and one-to-one contact with lower-performing students using the flipped approach as opposed to traditional methodologies. Other positive aspects as reported by students included the ability to assimilate content that might have been missed in class by being able to review, pause, rewind, and take down notes while watching videoed lessons; lower stress levels; and the ability to revisit the direct instruction component of the lesson at any time (Marlowe, 2012). Toppo (2011) looked at the work of a mathematics teacher who implemented a flipped approach. That teacher reported that his students achieved higher pass rates on exams and acquired more independence, and more class time became available for the teacher to review concepts and for and one-on-one practice with students. Other schools also have seen increases in student achievement after implementing the flipped approach (Duman, 2010; Fulton, 2012).

The flipped classroom is an excellent first step in making students' in-class experiences more active, more student centered, and more meaningful. Combining the best aspects of the flipped classroom with the power of 1:1 technology would allow for an even more radical reshaping of the classroom. School could become a place where students can learn at their own individual paces, become active content creators instead of solely passive content recipients, and learn in an environment that they "own," which adjusts rapidly to meet their learning needs and interests.

VIRTUAL LEARNING

Winston Churchill once said, "We shape our dwellings, and afterwards our dwellings shape us."

These words were very much on Laura Fleming's mind when she joined NMHS in 2013 as its library media specialist.

Every librarian knows just how important the characteristics of the library space can be to making users feel welcome and encourage them to make use of its facilities. In NMHS, Ms. Fleming found herself faced with an outdated library, a space that had been allowed to fade and deteriorate, and most definitely an environment that had not inspired the school's staff or students to make much use of the facility for a number of years. Ms. Fleming had long been committed to the notion that school libraries in the 21st century should comprise fluid, flexible learning spaces, and she immediately set about the task of transforming the physical environment of the library into one that was more conducive to its primary purpose (Fleming, 2015a).

Taking Churchill's quote as her starting point, she used the school community itself to help her make a series of initially small changes designed to freshen up the space and turn it into a place where staff and students wanted to spend time. Turning the physical space of the library into something much more attractive to the school community was, of course, a critical step, but she also then set about broadening and extending the concept of the building from its purely physical attributes and physical space out onto the web. She began to develop an exciting virtual space that also would contribute to learning success across the school. Ms. Fleming borrowed a phrase from Pixar, an organization that had inspired her in the past, and embarked on a journey to transform her library into a place that would become the heart of a *constant learning organization*.

To achieve their goal, Pixar brought to their own campus a combination of flexible, creative, and collaborative office spaces and a willingness to seek out answers proactively to new problems by using the ever-developing collective knowledge of the organization as a whole. Pixar knew that that no one, at any level, knows all the answers, so they found ways of continually tapping into the shared knowledge of the whole Pixar workforce. In NMHS, Ms. Fleming wanted to take a decisive step toward a similar objective by exploring the possibilities offered by 3-D virtual learning and collaboration in the cloud. She wanted to explore how 21st-century libraries can use the vibrant and burgeoning virtual terrain for face-to-face collaboration, and she wanted to see how collaboration could be embedded into the planning and the outcomes of instructional design and the learning processes in the school.

She overcame some resistance to ensure an always-open library, where teachers, students, data, and content come together to increase the speed, richness, and effectiveness of knowledge creation and knowledge transfer. In a similar vein, another company that inspired Ms. Fleming in her transformative task, was the T-shirt company Threadless, which "puts everyone in charge" and defines itself as primarily a community. Just as Threadless demonstrated to Ms. Fleming what can happen when you allow a company to become what its customers want it to be, so she wanted the NMHS library to become a place where students felt empowered to contribute to a dynamic learning community and in which they know they can learn as much from each other as they can from their teachers or from the books and other learning materials available to them. Ms. Fleming's aim was to create an ambience in which students and teachers felt able to show their interest and passion in whatever they were doing, letting them bring all their ideas, skills, and knowledge to the fore for the benefit of the whole school, and to feel free to demonstrate their creativity in myriad ways, sharing everything across the whole school community and indeed beyond.

With a growing fascination with the possibilities of teaching and learning in the cloud, Ms. Fleming's work was greatly influenced by Sugata Mitra's TED talks on how students can teach themselves and on building a school in the cloud. The cloud is a growing and increasingly rich environment that allows for both synchronous and asynchronous learning, attributes that Ms. Fleming and her team wanted and utilized. She wanted to make available the boundless possibilities that exist in the cloud, an abundant ecosystem of knowledge and activities, to the teaching and learning happening in the school. She established opportunities for students to use existing content, to participate in the creation of new content, and to collaborate with others, physically and virtually, nearby or anywhere across the globe, through their chosen media.

Using her own extended network, Ms. Fleming formed a partnership with a company called ProtonMedia, which provides essentially an enterprise solution called ProtoSphere, intended for, and already being used successfully by, corporations across the United States and beyond. She wanted to use their solution to explore the possibilities of 3-D virtual learning and collaboration in the cloud. ProtoSphere is an engaging and stimulating online world that enables students and data to come together productively, a world in which users (students and teachers) are represented by avatars. The partnership established ProtoSphere as a tool for face-to-face interaction in the virtual space, as an online adjunct to their interaction in the physical space of the school, with the aim of raising student achievement and improving student performance overall while enabling teachers to deliver their classes more efficiently and effectively. Classes and lessons were no longer constrained by the physical classroom or the school timetable.

With the help of the team at ProtonMedia, Ms. Fleming was able to create a student-centered virtual space where students and teachers had access to various technologies, digital and print resources, and productive spaces that offered scope for collaboration and creativity. They designed the virtual space with five rooms, including a theater, a hall, large meeting rooms, and different learning spaces. With a pilot group of teachers and students, Ms. Fleming explored how learning and teaching, communicating, and collaborating are different in a virtual environment from the kinds of interaction everyone knew so well from the physical school. Users' avatars were able to interact in various ways within the five "rooms," and the collaborative learning activities that happened there allowed students to improve their performance in different ways. And, of course, extending the learning culture into the virtual environment in this way also helped prepare students for their potential roles in the 21st-century workforce, in which many of them will be expected to communicate and collaborate virtually.

Ms. Fleming and her teaching colleagues were able to explore both the similarities and differences in pedagogy made possible in a virtual environment, with more emphasis on the differences becoming quickly apparent. In this environment they saw the role of the teacher shift to that of a facilitator of knowledge acquisition and to one in which the traditional role of teacher as the source of all knowledge became much less tenable. They found the virtual space to be much more participatory and somewhat less hierarchical than the regular classroom. For example, one best practice they implemented was to design experiences for the avatars to get up and move as much as possible around the virtual environment. Participating students were able to talk to each other, view their own and other's work, interact with presentation and media content, record notes, and access the web, all at the same time, from anywhere. In the virtual campus at NMHS, teachers taught students in real time in the same synchronous fashion that they had done in the physical classroom, but students were able to access learning materials and content asynchronously, in other words, enabling them to empower their own learning to take place anytime and from anywhere. This virtual learning space helped overcome barriers to collaboration and allowed students the ability to work on projects anytime or anyplace.

Together, the philosophy and principles Ms. Fleming borrowed from Pixar and Threadless, adapted to align with the needs of the school community, helped her transform her library into a constant learning organization. The virtual space helped to redefine learning at NMHS in ways that we could never have imagined a few years ago. The cloud certainly is proving to be a place of continuous, boundless, real-life learning.

In the wider world, cloud computing has quickly become an essential tool of collaboration and environment for collaboration, whether in the workplace or in school. A recent research report from the Center for Digital Education (2014) outlined "7 Reasons to Adopt Mobility and Cloud-Based Initiatives." These include the following:

1. Effectively engage today's "digital natives" and prepare them for modern, technology-focused careers

2. Create a seamless transition between in-class and at-home learning

3. Change the way students access and learn from information, providing a deeply engaging, student-driven, and personalized learning experience

4. Provide anytime, anywhere access to online learning resources, collaboration, and sharing

5. Level the playing field for students who don't have access to computers or broadband Internet access at home

6. Eliminate the need to carry around or purchase textbooks

7. Provide access to always-current learning materials and resources

In addition to cloud-based virtual learning, expanded opportunities can be provided to students through asynchronous options. These options vary from state to state as some have their own virtual learning schools for students to tap into. A general option that is open to all schools is the Virtual High School (VHS; http://www.thevhscollaborative.org/). For a subscription fee, schools can expand student access to advanced placement (AP) and specialized elective courses to complement what is already available. By integrating, VHS leaders can expand academic options to students in upward of 230 diverse courses. At NMHS we allowed students to either substitute a VHS course for a face-to-face elective option or add an additional class to their current load. In the latter case all work had to be completed outside of school.

IMPLEMENTATION TIPS

- Ensure infrastructure and necessary technology resources are in place. Secure funding if needed, or allocate funds in current budget.
- Educate staff on blended and virtual learning models.
- Provide support in the form of professional learning.
- Make sure desired learning outcomes are identified and how they will be assessed.
- Monitor and provide feedback options to ensure they are being implemented effectively.

SUMMARY

Blended and virtual learning opportunities provide uncommon experiences for students that add personalization, individualization, differentiation, and pacing that cater to the needs of all learners. They enhance traditional pedagogical techniques while expanding opportunities available to students both in and out of school. As a result these initiatives provide more relevancy for students as they are afforded the opportunity to take more ownership over their learning while being motivated by choice. As schools begin to experiment with blended and virtual learning pilot programs or classroom projects, a vision and plan for expansion across the entire system should be developed, so all kids experience the benefits outlined in this chapter.

Bring Your Own Device (BYOD)

Technology seems to be more accessible than ever before. It is common to walk into a typical household these days and see a variety of devices being charged. One of the first things I look for when I go to a friend's house is whether or not any charging cables are readily available in case I need one. Even when we entertain guests, I will go to charge my iPhone and find that someone has already commandeered my charger, much to my chagrin. Many people regularly take some sort of charging apparatus with them wherever they go. Access to technology is by no means isolated only to adults. As devices have become more affordable over the years, parents have bestowed a variety of mobile technologies upon their children. We really are living in a digital age.

As a result of the advances in technology and an increase in Wi-Fi access, schools have slowly begun to respond to this trend. The realization now is that many students possess devices, and it only makes sense to harness and leverage their immense power. For many, even the most stubborn school districts that have fought this trend for years have begun to change course. All one has to do is look to the largest school district in the United States, the New York City public school system, to see that they have just lifted a 10-year ban on students bringing their cell phones to school. The potential is there for schools and educators to empower students to take more ownership of their learning. This has resulted in a growing trend of bring your own device (BYOD) initiatives being adopted. This has been the preferred option as opposed to 1:1 initiatives due to overall cost.

THE DEVICE CONUNDRUM—1:1 VERSUS BYOD

Schools and districts are beginning to rethink pedagogy and learning environments by instituting either 1:1 device programs or BYOD initiatives. In my opinion, schools that wish to create the most relevant and meaningful learning culture will go in one of these directions. It is tough to argue the potential impact of either program, implemented diligently and with a focus on learning, that will not result in the enhancement of essential skill sets that our students need to succeed in today's digital world. Probably the most significant impact either 1:1 or BYOD can have is in the area of teaching digital responsibility, citizenship, and the creation of positive footprints online. After all, in the real world that we are preparing our students for, technological literacies and proficiencies are the cornerstones of numerous career paths.

The decision on which way to go is usually determined by finances, which is unfortunate for those schools and districts that have their hearts set on getting a device in the hands of each and every student. Competition resulting from the continuous evolution of tablets, laptops, and now Chromebooks, puts schools in a better position to make large-scale investments in mobile technology. In theory and on paper, a 1:1 program seems to be the best for schools wanting to integrate technology on a macro level to enhance teaching and learning. Advocates for 1:1 programs will claim that it is the only way to go as it ensures equitable access to all students regardless of socioeconomic status.

With each student possessing a device, collaborative work using Web 2.0 tools is a reality for all students, both in an out of school, provided there is Internet access at home. In this day and age, finding a location with free Wi-Fi is not such a difficult task. Maintenance becomes less of a headache for the IT department as they only have to worry about one type of device. It also figures to entail a more streamlined approach when it comes to providing professional development to staff so that the devices are consistently utilized to support student learning.

The general case for 1:1 programs is compelling, but is it the best option for our students today? The more I read about others' thoughts on this and reflect on the BYOD program we have instituted at New Milford High School (NMHS), I am beginning to think that 1:1 programs are not necessarily the best option for our students. My main reason for this shift in thought is this: why would we want to pigeonhole our students to one single device or platform? Is that reminiscent of the real world that we are supposedly preparing them to flourish and succeed in? The fact is that many students own and are comfortable with their devices. The digital divide in schools becomes smaller when bold districts, schools, and educators work to effectively integrate the technology that has been available for years outside their walls. BYOD has the ability to save districts money, but the real impact comes in the form or engagement and empowerment of students to learn on their terms. I have grown quite tired of the myriad of excuses to not move toward BYOD because it can and will have a positive impact with the right mind-set, training, and support.

It makes sense to me to create a technology-rich learning environment that leverages available technology that the students already own. This is what we have done at my school and experienced a great deal of success. In addition to BYOD, students and teachers have access to three PC labs, one iMac lab, one MacBook cart, one PC cart, and one netbook cart. The equity issue with BYOD in classrooms has been overcome with school-purchased technology and the use of cooperative learning after my teachers determine which device(s) each student possesses and brings to school on a regular basis. In my eyes we are accomplishing the same goals, for the most part, as we would if a 1:1 program had been instituted. Students have access to technology and are using it on a daily basis to communicate, collaborate, create artifacts of learning, problem solve, think critically, become more technologically proficient, and develop a greater global awareness. They should most certainly be able to use it to replace more archaic forms of technology (i.e., pencil and paper) if they wish.

SUCCESS IN RURAL AMERICA

St. Paul Schools, a rural, isolated, K–12 school in Arkansas, serves a student body of whom more than 80 percent receive free or reduced lunch. When Daisy Dyer-Duerr took charge as principal in 2011, St. Paul was a failing school, with lackluster test scores and falling enrollment, on the verge of being taken over by the state. Four years later, it is brimming with technology and ranked in the top 10 percent of Arkansas schools (Berdik, 2015).

During the summer of 2011 the last thing on Mrs. Dyer-Duerr's mind was winning awards, much less becoming a featured school for Digital Learning Day in 2015 (Dyer-Duerr, personal communication, 2015). She was merely focused on the *survival* of her new school. St. Paul Schools was a campus riddled with failure—a school on year two of state-mandated school improvement for both literacy and math (due to poor test scores) that had suffered eight consecutive years of declining enrollment and was at risk of being shut down by both its home school district and the state of Arkansas.

Obviously the tide had to change and change quickly if this rural, isolated Arkansas school was going to survive.

Mrs. Dyer-Duerr's immediate plans involved input and ownership from all stakeholders integral in the success of the school. Teachers, staff members, parents, students, and community members were brought together to form a "Vision for Success" for St. Paul Schools. This was a new concept welcomed with both surprise and awe in the community. The result was a comprehensive vision with two main components: St. Paul Schools would focus on: "(a) integration of technology and (b) relationships with all students." These would be the guiding principles of a "rebirth" of St. Paul Schools. A new "culture" of "no excuses . . . no limits" was ingrained within the school and community; this has led to an unbelievable success story (Dyer-Duerr, 2015).

Mrs. Dyer-Duerr points to commitment by all stakeholders and the implementation of various programs that have led to a three-year turnaround at St. Paul Schools. One of the most influential programs Mrs. Dyer-Duerr speaks of is the adoption of a BYOD program in the 2012-to-2013 school year. "This was not a conventional adoption by any means" (Dyer-Duerr, 2015). Her school district was what she refers to as a "lock down" district—students who were even seen with a cell phone in school were immediately assigned to three days of in-school suspension, and that was for a first offense. Parents also were required to pick up their cell phones from the office. This was a daunting task for Mrs. Dyer-Duerr as principal as she was the only administrator within 30 miles; to say this rule caused problems with school–parent–community relationships would be a huge understatement.

Meanwhile, in the spring of 2012, Mrs. Dyer-Duerr applied (and received) a 21st Century Community Learning Center Grant. Part of the application process required intensive surveying of staff, community members, parents, and students. One of the extremely enlightening results of this survey was that only 10 percent of St. Paul students' homes were equipped with Internet access, and some of these homes were still using dial-up Internet. "From this survey I embarrassingly made the assumption many do about low SES students; they don't have access to cell phones or electronic devices" (Dyer-Duerr, 2015). After about two months of the 2012 school year, Mrs. Dyer-Duerr began to question her assumption. "I thought to myself: I sure am punishing a lot of these low-SES students for having cell phones. Something has to be wrong with my thinking" (Dyer-Duerr, 2015). At this point she took a survey of her high school; this involved all students in Grades 7 through 12. The results of this survey were shocking to Mrs. Dyer-Duerr. Just over 75 percent of these students had cell phones, and over half of these cell phones were smartphones. Mrs. Dyer-Duerr was *shocked*! This totally changed her perception of what could be done in St. Paul Schools. To her this meant it no longer had to be about finding devices for every student because as Mrs. Dyer-Duerr said, "The devices were right there—in their pockets!"

Mrs. Dyer-Duerr took this newfound information to her school board and lobbied for a BYOD policy for her school. This was somewhat of a tough sell because the other five campuses (all much richer) did not have this in place and were not interested at all in an initiative like this. Mrs. Dyer-Duerr also immediately contacted me to get information regarding a BYOD agreement; she was able to modify the one I used at NMHS to meet the needs of St. Paul High School.

Other concerns were (a) bandwidth, (b) teacher training, and (c) student, parent, and community input. Mrs. Dyer-Duerr said teaching teachers to utilize BYOD is still something they are working on at St. Paul Schools. Some teachers are amazing with this tool, some are still scared of the tool, but more than anything, they always now have enough devices for their students. She says bandwidth is a constant battle as a rural, isolated school. She actually testified in front of the Federal Communications Commission (FCC) in November of 2014 when the FCC voted to expand E-rate spending. She said getting to tell the importance of access to Internet for all students, regardless of their location, to those who are making decisions in Washington was an amazing experience. Her local school board did approve BYOD for St. Paul Schools and since late in

2012, her low-SES, isolated, rural school has been operating a successful BYOD program. She claims the day the "cell phone lockdown" was lifted was probably her most popular day as a principal with her students and parents. Students are now empowered by the ability to use their own devices. Her students have told her they feel more trusted, valued, and involved in their educations now that they are allowed to use their personal devices in school. Discipline referrals are down, and the divide that was causing problems with the parent–school relationship is now gone.

Mrs. Dyer-Duerr emphasizes the importance of constantly improving the instruction and way BYOD is utilized in her school's classrooms. Most importantly she emphasizes that low-SES and location are *not* something that should ever "hold administrators or schools back from empowering students with BYOD." Mrs. Dyer-Duerr believes that if we truly want authentic student voice, we need to allow them to use the device of their choice (Dyer-Duerr, 2015).

Since the approval of the new vision with an emphasis on technology integration and relationships along with the adoption of a BYOD program in 2012, St. Paul Schools has gone from a failing school to in 2014 being a "Top 10% School in Arkansas." St. Paul Schools also has been recognized as a "Model School" by the International Center for Leadership in Education in 2014. St. Paul Schools also has been recognized as an "Exemplar Feature School" for Digital Learning Day 2015. Don't ever tell Daisy Dyer-Duerr students can't be successful because they are too poor or they live somewhere that keeps them from having access to a great education; her school can prove you wrong.

The Elements of a Successful BYOD Initiative

Many schools and districts that have adopted BYOD have done so without proper planning and support. The overall goal of any BYOD initiative should be to support and enhance student learning. It should not be implemented as a way to pacify students by allowing them to use their devices only during noninstructional time or to eliminate discipline issues. Don't get me wrong; I believe that these are two important outcomes of BYOD but firmly believe that student-owned devices in school have to be aligned to learning outcomes first and foremost. Other important outcomes on behalf of the student include increasing productivity, conducting better research, becoming more digitally literate, and developing into a digitally responsible citizen. BYOD begins with trusting and respecting students. The fact remains though that the cart is too often placed before the horse—a rash decision is made to go BYOD without a sound rationale for how it will impact student learning. The following are key drivers of a successful BYOD initiative:

1. **Infrastructure.** Herein lies a common pitfall for many schools and districts that implement BYOD. Before going any further, it is pivotal to ensure that the infrastructure can withstand the stress of mobile technologies accessing the Wi-Fi network. You need to expect that there will be more devices connected to the network on a given day than there are students. Not only will some students bring in more than one device, but you have to account for staff member access as well. There is nothing worse than developing and implementing a lesson that integrates mobile learning devices than to have the Internet slowed down to a snail's pace. Or even worse, the network crashes or begins to negatively impact teachers and students using school-owned mobile technology.

2. **Shared Vision.** This is extremely important as you will have staff and community members on both sides of the fence. Before going full steam ahead with BYOD, gather key stakeholders to establish a shared vision that includes rationale, goals, expected outcomes, expectations, and means to assess the effectiveness of

the initiative. Central to a BYOD vision is a consistent focus on student learning.

3. **Strategic Plan.** The shared vision that is created by all stakeholder representatives, including students, will drive a plan for action. As is the case in any successful initiative, sound planning is imperative. During the planning process one must consider community outreach, budget allocations to improve existing infrastructure, policies, professional development (teacher and administrator), student trainings, and evaluation procedures (i.e., how do I know that this is impacting student learning?). Sound pedagogy must be at the heart of any BYOD initiative.

4. **Policy Development.** Part of the strategic planning process will be to develop policies and procedures relating to BYOD. It is important that the resulting artifacts are not too overbearing and afford students the opportunity to be trusted and empowered to take ownership of their learning. A sound policy addresses Wi-Fi login procedures, a focus on learning, acceptable use, and absolving the school of any liability for lost, stolen, or broken devices.

5. **Professional Development.** As I work with schools and districts across the country on BYOD initiatives, I can honestly say that this is one area where mistakes are made. Teachers need proper support in terms of developing pedagogically sound lessons, designing assessments aligned to higher standards, exposure to web-based tools and apps that cater to BYOD, ensuring equity, and developing classroom procedures. Prior to rolling out a school-or district-wide BYOD initiative, teachers should know full well what the outcomes are as articulated in the shared vision and have a set of tools and instructional strategies that can be used on the first day. Another key to success is ongoing professional development to provide teachers with additional

strategies and ideas so that devices are used to support learning. In addition to teachers, leaders also need professional development in regard to the observation and evaluation process. They are the ones after all that have to make sure that mobile devices are being used properly to support learning while addressing higher standards. Before implementing BYOD as a school or district, make sure professional development has been provided to teachers and administrators.

6. **Student Programs.** Students themselves need a form of professional development on the expectations and outcomes of device use. Successful initiatives contain an embedded component that includes educational programs for students before a BYOD initiative is rolled out and ones that are continued each year. These programs, which can be held once in the beginning of the school year, focus on how devices should be used to support learning as well as digital responsibility. As principal, I held annual assemblies in the early fall for each grade level, that focused on cyberbullying, creating positive digital footprints, and the tenets of our BYOD program. The end result was that our students embraced the shared vision, and device use was more focused on learning than off-task behavior. We were also in a better position to give up control and trust our kids.

7. **Budget Allocations.** Although BYOD initiatives are a cost-effective means to increase student access to technology in school, there are solutions available to help streamline teaching and learning devices. ClassLink Launchpad is a fantastic learning management system (LMS) that can be purchased to deliver a uniform experience across all devices to assist with the teaching and learning. With ClassLink students and teachers can access a customized dashboard that is preloaded with a variety of tools that are used on a regular basis. Some teachers have even used it to help transform their classrooms into paperless environments.

By focusing on these elements, BYOD can be implemented successfully in your school or district with the primary focus being on student learning. For the latest resources, sample policies, and lesson ideas visit http://www.pinterest.com/esheninger/byod/.

A Focus on Learning

Mobile learning provides enhanced collaboration among learners, access to information, and a deeper contextualization of learning. Hypothetically, effective mobile learning can empower learners by enabling them to better assess and select relevant information, redefine their goals, and reconsider their understanding of concepts within a shifting and growing frame of reference (the information context).

—Marguerite L. Koole (2009)

The current wide spread of mobile devices and wireless technologies brings an enormous potential to e-learning in terms of ubiquity, pervasiveness, personalization, and flexibility (Caballé, Xhafa, & Barolli, 2010). Any device initiative, whether 1:1 or BYOD, should squarely focus on student learning. Learning theories and frameworks that present the operational, goal-oriented outcomes are great starting points for educators looking to incorporate mobile learning initiatives and student activities. Futurelab (2004) outlined six broad theory-based categories of activity that compromise successful mobile learning initiatives. These key drivers will assist you in developing a shared vision and strategic plan for BYOD implementation:

- **Behaviorist.** Activities that promote learning as a change in learners' observable actions—in the behaviorist paradigm, learning is thought to be best facilitated through the reinforcement of an association between a particular stimulus and a response. Applying this to educational technology, mobile-aided learning is the presentation of a problem (stimulus) followed by the contribution on the part of the learner of the solution (response). Feedback from the system then provides the reinforcement. In the context of mobile learning, using devices as student-response systems with apps such as Poll Everywhere, would align to this category.

- Constructivist. Activities in which learners actively construct new ideas or concepts based on both their previous and current knowledge—in this approach, learning is an active process in which learners construct new ideas or concepts based on both their current and past knowledge. They are encouraged to be active constructors of knowledge, with mobile devices placing them in a realistic context at the same time as offering access to supporting tools. Jantjies and Joy (2013) found that the opportunity of being able to create material in their own languages on their own mobile phones at their own time allowed learners to create learning material that they could relate to and engage with at any time.

- Situated. Activities that promote learning within an authentic context and culture—learning can be enhanced by ensuring that it takes place in an authentic context (Herrington & Kervin, 2007). Authentic learning experiences should (a) focus on practical, lifelike problems that imitate the trade of experts in the field with communication of results to individuals outside the classroom, (b) be inquiry based with an emphasis on metacognitive skills, (c) encourage learners to participate in active conversations in a social learning environment, and (d) allow learners make choices and guide their own learning in meaningful, task-oriented work (Rule, 2006). Today's technological resources can make authentic learning more practical and easier to implement than ever before (Lombardi, 2007). Mobile devices are especially well suited to context-aware applications simply because they are available in different contexts and so can draw on those contexts to enhance the learning activity.

- **Collaborative.** Activities that promote learning through social interaction—Caballé et al. (2010) found that mobile technology can offer new opportunities for groups of learners to collaborate inside and beyond the traditional instructor-oriented educational paradigm. There is an array of applications, such as Google Apps, Padlet, Edmodo, and TodaysMeet, that can be accessed easily on mobile devices and that educators can seamlessly integrate into BYOD learning activities to promote collaboration.

- **Informal and Lifelong.** Activities that support learning outside a dedicated learning environment and formal curriculum—informal and lifelong learning happens all of the time and is influenced both by our environment and the particular situations we are faced with. Informal learning may be intentional, for example, through intensive, significant, and deliberate learning "projects" (Tough, 1971), or it may be accidental, by acquiring information through conversations, TV, and media; observing the world; or even experiencing an accident or embarrassing situation. As such, learning becomes embedded in everyday life, thus emphasizing the value of mobile technologies in supporting it. With access to the Internet, educators can promote and enhance both informal and lifelong learning among students with ease when mobile devices are integrated effectively.

- **Learning and Teaching Support.** Activities that assist in the coordination of learners and resources for learning activities—education as a process relies on a great deal of coordination of learners and resources. Mobile devices can be used by teachers to access student information, grades, and schedules. They also can use them to access information specific to them contained in calendars, online documents, and apps. Mobile devices can be leveraged to provide learning activities and course material to students, including due dates for assignments and information about timetable and room changes. Formative and summative assessments can easily be created and administered to students using free tools. For example, a teacher could assign a paper in Google Docs where he or she could provide real-time feedback. Google Forms could be configured as a self-grading quiz. A blended approach to enabling learning with mobile devices is a sound approach as successful and engaging activities draw on a number of different theories and practices.

Koole's (2009) Framework for the Rational Analysis of Mobile Education (FRAME) model provides a more holistic framework for mobile learning. It is composed of a three-circle Venn diagram comprising the learner aspect (L), the social aspect (S), and the device aspect (D). The learner aspect (L) takes into account a student's cognitive abilities, memory, prior knowledge, emotions, and possible motivations. This aspect describes how learners use what they already know and how they encode, store, and transfer information. This aspect also draws upon learning theories regarding knowledge transfer and learning by discovery. The social aspect (S) takes into account the processes of social interaction and cooperation. Students must follow the rules of cooperation to communicate, which enables them to exchange information, acquire knowledge, and sustain cultural practices. The device aspect (D) refers to the physical, technical, and functional characteristics of a mobile device. The physical characteristics include input and output capabilities as well as processes internal to the machine such as storage capabilities, power, processor speed, compatibility, and expandability.

In this framework, mobile learning is a combination of the interactions among learners, their devices, and other people. Koole provides a useful checklist that schools and educators can refer to when looking to integrate mobile

Figure 6.1

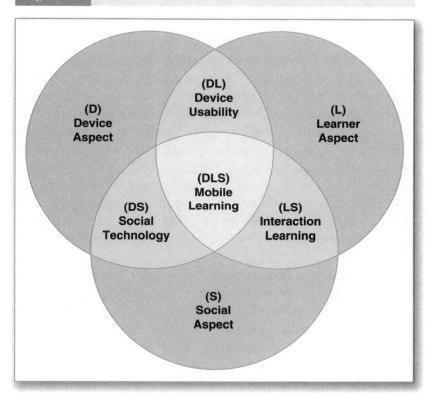

learning effectively as part of a BYOD initiative. Koole (2009) asks if you have considered the following in your mobile learning ecosystem:

1. How use of mobile devices might change the process of interactions among learners, communities, and systems

2. How learners may most effectively use mobile access to other learners, systems, and devices to recognize and evaluate information and processes to achieve their goals

3. How learners can become more independent in navigating through and filtering information

4. How the roles of teachers and learners will change and how to prepare them for that change

Effective mobile learning, the primary intersection of the FRAME model, results from the integration of the device (D), learner (L), and social (S) aspects. Mobile learning provides enhanced collaboration among learners, access to information, and a deeper contextualization of learning. It also can empower learners by enabling them to better assess and select relevant information, redefine their goals, and reconsider their understanding of concepts within a shifting and growing frame of reference within an informational context. Effective mobile learning provides an enhanced cognitive environment in which learners can better interact with their instructors, content, their physical and virtual environments, and each other (Koole, 2009).

Mobile devices offer a new and exciting avenue to engage students and promote learning while increasing academic achievement. Research by Cristol and Gimbert (2013) found that students utilizing mobile learning devices scored, on average, 52.34 points higher on the state assessments than their peers who did not use them. Students are more connected than ever with their devices, and it is necessary for teachers to capitalize on this opportunity to drive student learning and outcomes. History teacher Hershey Groff encourages students to bring in their mobile devices on a daily basis as he incorporates them in wide range of activities aimed at promoting learning. He uses mobile apps such as Socrative and Poll Everywhere in various capacities including quick-write prompts, image analysis, and student "space races," where teams of students answer questions in a fast-paced rocket race game and get their rockets the furthest across the screen to win. Other programs like Remind also help promote classroom achievement as short message service (SMS) text messages and e-mails can be sent to students to keep them up-to-date on class activities and assignments.

Mr. Groff advocates that students use tablets, laptops, and cell phones to take class notes or work on projects with programs like Evernote or Google Docs, so they can be shared and edited as needed. This alleviates the problem of students leaving necessary work at home and opens up new avenues of communication and collaboration. He strongly believes that mobile devices offer an excellent opportunity to drive student inquiry and research-based projects because they allow students to experience large amounts of content from a wide variety of primary and secondary sources.

MOVING TOWARD A PAPERLESS ENVIRONMENT

At NMHS teachers have adapted their professional practice as the culture continues to evolve into a BYOD school where student-owned technology is integrated effectively. The BYOD environment allowed Vikki Smith's science class to go paperless. Students complete assignments—whether it's homework, class work, projects, or tests all online using various Web sites, such as Edmodo, Tumblr, and Instagram—on their BYOD devices. They also use their smartphones, iPads, iPods, and digital cameras to take notes or to capture information. All pictures, notes, and assignments are posted on the Web sites, e-mailed, or placed on their private homework blogs. This has led to more student engagement, accountability, and participation in the classroom; peer reviews; and instant feedback to the students on how they are progressing.

In chemistry, marine biology, and bioethics studies, every week each student makes two reflective and analytical posts on their blogs using either Tumblr, WordPress, Blogger, Pinterest, or Weebly to explore what has been happening globally or locally, either on TV or the Internet, and then making connections to what they have been learning in class. Ms. Smith provides the students with choice, which has allowed each of them to take more ownership over what they are interested in and want to learn about in science. Students also used Instagram as a communication tool (like texting) as a way to give feedback, make comments, and reflect on what they have been learning. This works extremely well in bioethical studies, where some students may be reluctant and shy to express their opinions. One topic had 143 comments in the 48-minute period. Using Instagram allowed everyone to have a voice and be heard. They have also used Instagram and Webstagram to send short videos when Ms. Smith has been absent to show they have been engaged, completing their work, and staying on task. BYOD makes all of this possible.

Ensuring Equity

With the growing access that students now have to technology at home, educators are seizing this opportunity to increase access in the classroom. For cash-strapped districts BYOD seems like the logical solution to leverage the mobile devices students have to enhance learning, increase productivity, conduct better research, address critical digital literacies, and teach digital responsibility. In theory this all sounds fantastic, and there are many benefits that I have witnessed firsthand after successfully implementing a BYOD initiative more than five years ago at my high school. However, in practice it is important to ensure that any initiative involving student-owned devices is well thought out with a resulting plan for action focused on student learning. For more information on how to implement a successful BYOD initiative, make sure all of these drivers discussed in the chapter are firmly in place.

One issue that comes up frequently with BYOD initiatives is equity. The equity issue either haunts those who have or are in the process of going BYOD. There are other times, however, that this issue stops the initiative from moving forward. In any case the ones who suffer are our students. In today's digital age, who are we to tell students that they cannot bring their tools to class to support learning? Don't get me wrong; equity is a real issue that needs to be addressed when rolling out or sustaining any BYOD initiative. It is our job as leaders and educators to provide the best possible learning environment for our students. With this being said the equity issue should not be seen as an obstacle or challenge that cannot be overcome. Instead of using this as an excuse, or allowing the naysayers to use this as ammunition to derail the initiative, it is our job to find applicable solutions to create schools that work for today's learners. After all, it is not about our (adult) learning but our students.

In my community where we made the decision to roll out BYOD many years ago, we did so knowing full well that all of our students did not own a device. Through our planning we also discovered that some students had parents or guardians who would not allow them to bring them to school for fear of theft or breakage. Then there was a small group of students who flat out told us that they had no interest in using their technology in school to support learning. All of these challenges could have been excuses not to move forward, but we decided to find some solutions to benefit the majority while not excluding any student. Any successful BYOD initiative should focus squarely on how students can use mobile devices to support their learning. If a lesson called for every student to use a device to demonstrate conceptual mastery aligned to a specific learning outcome, it was our job to ensure this. Here are some practical tips that we utilized to ensure BYOD equity:

1. **Know Your Students.** Once a decision has been made to implement BYOD in your school or district and proper professional development has been provided, find out who are the haves and have-nots. One suggestion is to use Google Forms to curate this information. Going forward this will allow you to focus on those students who need access.

2. **Advance Planning.** Notify students the day before that they will need to bring their device to class the following day if the learning activity calls for it.

3. **Supplement School Technology.** If a learning activity calls for every student to have a device, then it is imperative

that supports are put in place. Students will either forget to bring their device, not have one, or choose not to bring it into school. A successful BYOD initiative has ample technology on hand to make sure all students have access to tools.

4. **Utilize Cooperative Learning.** This archaic pedagogical technique is a necessity in a BYOD environment. There will be some cases where supplemental school technology is not available. Developing lessons where collaborative groups are established and all students have equitable access to a mobile device to accomplish the learning outcome is a sound practice.

5. **Engage Parents.** Prior to going BYOD, parent meetings should be planned and held to discuss the initiative as well as outcomes and expectations. These conversations also clearly should outline how the issue of equity will be handled.

Device envy is another issue that is commonly referenced by critics as a reason for not implementing BYOD. As children we all experienced some sort of envious situation in school. For me personally it is when I wanted Air Jordan sneakers, and my parents bought me Converse. Sure, it didn't make me feel good, but I learned to deal with it. Part of preparing our students for life is helping them to deal with envy in positive ways. As educators the last thing we want to do is make students feel bad about the types of devices they have, but we also don't want to use this excuse to exclude the potential of mobile learning. The best way to avoid any envious situation is to keep the focus on learning. Not only did we do this, but we also began signing out school-owned technology to students who did not have access at all. When it was all said and done, we never received one complaint from our parents on the equity or envy issues.

IMPLEMENTATION TIPS

- Conduct an infrastructure audit to ensure there is enough bandwidth and access points to support device use by all students and staff.
- Develop a shared vision and plan for action that focuses on learning. Resulting policies should connect to existing acceptable use policies and reflect a commitment to learning.
- Provide initial professional development prior to the rollout, and ensure ongoing training and support is provided thereafter.
- Provide ongoing student and parent presentations to reinforce the objectives of the initiative.

SUMMARY

Students today possess an array of powerful tools that can be harnessed and leveraged by schools to provide more relevant learning opportunities. BYOD initiatives that focus on learning have the potential to not only increase engagement but also achievement. By focusing on the elements of establishing a successful BYOD initiative in this chapter, schools will open up endless possibilities for leaners to engage in deeper, more meaningful learning while teaching them critical digital literacies and citizenship in the process. If the goal of schools is to prepare students for the real world, then they should be empowered to use the very same tools that will be expected of them in the career paths that they choose.

Digital Badging and Micro-Credentials

For a person to remain competitive in today's workforce, there must be continual learning. In order to capture the many and often informal ways that students and workers acquire knowledge and skills, and to enable institutions to recognize their accomplishments, we must embrace a more modern and comprehensive credentialing system.

—Former President Bill Clinton
(Reconnect Learning, 2014)

DIGITAL BADGING TO SUPPORT PROFESSIONAL LEARNING

Badging has a long and venerable history. It has been a familiar concept since long before the first mention of digital badges was made. They have a long, rich history that goes back as far as the Middle Ages. Law enforcement badges denote areas of law enforcement and rank. Scouts have more than 130 merit badges that they can earn. A scout will choose a badge in an area of activity that is of interest to him or her and will then fulfill the requirements for that badge to earn it. "In the digital era, we have even seen badges used in gaming and in a variety of other online spaces to motivate behavior, recognize achievement and establish credibility" (Fleming, 2015a).

Today we live in a time where content is ubiquitous. Learning today can happen anytime and anywhere—on the job, in the community, or online. This fact was recognized by Laura Fleming, the library media specialist at New Milford High School (NMHS), who came to the school with the idea that the world is our platform (Fleming, 2015a). Like many school librarians, Ms. Fleming plays a leadership role in her school's professional development initiatives. Her journey into the world of digital badging started in 2013 with a challenge from me to develop an innovative system that would familiarize teachers with Web 2.0 tools and related technologies. Ms. Fleming had long seen that education and the workplace were changing and was challenged and stimulated by the possibility of, on the one hand, recognizing and valuing the many and varied ways that educators are able to learn today, and on the other hand, coming up with a method that would best capture and communicate that knowledge.

Having developed, over recent years, a professional interest in leveraging the power of multiple platforms to reach and engage all learners in this digital age, Ms. Fleming had come to the school with an already active interest in digital badges but had until this point viewed them as an initiative focused on student learning and informal credentialing. However, she also brought with her the knowledge that any such program of digital badging for students was likely to fall flat unless their teachers understood and appreciated the value of digital badges. So, Ms. Fleming decided, what better way to give NMHS teachers that appreciation than to let them experience digital badging for themselves in relation to their own professional development?

It was at that point she decided to marry the two ideas into a digital-badge-based professional learning platform. The platform would provide professional learning opportunities for teachers and give them firsthand experience with a digital-badge-based learning system. "I was 16 years into my own career as an educator, with a firm understanding of what worked in teacher professional learning and what didn't, and I was ready to disrupt the system!" (Fleming, 2015a).

But why digital badges? Digital badges can be used to guide, motivate, and validate informal learning. Acknowledging the informal learning of educators had been a long-neglected area in schools, and Ms. Fleming felt she could make a big impact there. She felt that a digital-badge-based system would allow participating educators to learn and earn badges anytime and anywhere. Educators could then use those badges to build and communicate their own reputations to their colleagues and to senior staff, capturing a complete picture of their own professional development for others to see (Fleming, 2015a).

In the relatively short time that digital badges have been used in education, they have been defined, created, and issued by a broad range of institutions, initiatives, and projects, including formal and informal educational institutions, after-school programs, groups focusing on professional development, and many more besides. It starts from the very simple premise that anyone can earn a badge for doing something useful by evidencing what has been done so that the evidence can be assessed. Earners can then display their badges on Web sites, blogs, social media profiles and networks, portfolios, and résumés. Based on these principles, Ms. Fleming went to work on developing a groundbreaking credentialing system to acknowledge the informal learning of educators.

Ms. Fleming has always been a strong advocate of Mozilla's powerful philosophy and has tried to shape much of her own career around their idea of making the Internet open and participatory. Just a quick glance at the first few principles in the Mozilla Manifesto (http://www.mozilla.org/en-US/about/manifesto/) makes their philosophy plain:

- The Internet is an integral part of modern life—a key component in education, communication, collaboration, business, entertainment, and society as a whole.
- The Internet is a global public resource that must remain open and accessible.

The manifesto explains that the Internet is becoming an increasingly important part of our lives and that openness, innovation, and opportunity are key to the continued health of the Internet.

From this starting point, Ms. Fleming had a vision for the platform but faced a steep learning curve to make it happen. She started with a company called Credly and a WordPress plug-in that they produced called BadgeOS. Credly is a free web service for issuing, earning, and sharing badges. BadgeOS instantly transforms a WordPress Web site into a platform for recognizing achievement. She knew she had found the solution, and although she had only basic familiarity with WordPress, she refused to let that stop her. "I purchased a domain name, *www.worlds-of-learning-nmhs.com* in the hope that other schools might want a similar system of learning for their teachers and be able to substitute their own school name for NMHS—New Milford High School" (Fleming, 2015a).

The next step was to design the badges for the platform. To be credible, digital badges must include information, as metadata, about when and how they were earned and who issued them. They provide a digital hyperlink to information about the badge's associated skills and the projects or tasks that the badge holder has completed to earn it. Ms. Fleming developed the badges for the platform based on the open badge standard (http://www.openbadges.org), a clear set of metadata allocated to each badge, which can include the following:

- issuer information
- earner information

- criteria
- evidence
- standards alignment

By October of 2013, she was ready and able to launch Worlds of Learning @ New Milford High School, a digital-badge-based professional learning platform.

Worlds of Learning @ New Milford High School provides a framework that allows teachers to earn digital badges through learning about a range of technology tools and applications and then putting what they learn into practice in their own teaching. The platform has been designed so that its resources will help to prepare educators to fully leverage the potential for mastering digital-age skills as embodied in the International Society for Technology in Education (ISTE) Standards for Teachers as well as assisting them to achieve the seamless integration of technology as addressed by the Common Core State Standards. As technology convergence and integration continues to increase generally in our society, it is paramount that teachers possess the skills and behaviors of digital-age professionals. Educators should be comfortable teaching, working, and learning in an increasingly connected global digital society. The real aim of educational technology should be to modernize pedagogy and to shape the education of the future. Registered users on the Worlds of Learning site can take the tools presented on the platform and integrate them seamlessly into meaningful learning that addresses the standards in their respective content areas.

Ms. Fleming tried to streamline the user experience on the platform as much as possible. Teachers (or indeed anyone who wants to join) simply register on the platform. Members can then choose to learn about a tool from among the (growing) selection of badges she has on the site. Her badges include those for mastering tools like Buncee (http://www.buncee .com), Padlet (http://www.padlet.com), and ThingLink (http://www.thinglink.com) as well as a variety of other web-based tools.

To learn about each tool, Ms. Fleming provides a deliberately brief description of what the tool is. She also includes a very short screencast that provides an overview of how to use each tool and a brief written description of how the tool can be used and how the tool can be integrated effectively into the curriculum through the Common Core. Educators can earn the badge by then assimilating what they've learned into their own instruction in some way. Users submit "proof" to her that they have done so. Their evidence might consist of a web link to a page or site that demonstrates what they have done, a lesson plan, a video of classroom practice, or even a text description of how they or their students have used the tool. Upon receiving documentation, she issues a digital badge for their learning.

After her very first Tweet to promote the platform, Ms. Fleming was thrilled to see that not only did teachers in her district join but so did teachers from all over the country and even some internationally. The feedback Ms. Fleming received was tremendous. She was inundated with e-mails thanking her for developing such a system, and she also received messages from educators and administrators asking her how they could develop a similar system. At that point, further inspired by Mozilla efforts, she decided to bundle her WordPress files into a package for districts, or any others for that matter, to be able to install and personalize the system for themselves. Some districts expressed interest in integrating the badging system exactly as Ms. Fleming developed it, whereas others wanted to take the platform, add in their own components, and use it as a springboard into badging in other areas. Examples of the latter include online academy classes, information literacy skills, training library staff, and recognizing the digital achievements of students and staff in 1:1 initiatives. With the success of the platform not only at the school level, NMHS is now officially a participating issuer of open badges. Ms. Fleming creates, issues, and verifies digital badges for educators all around the world.

In the words of one educator who contacted Ms. Fleming:

"I think your platform is exactly what my school needs to motivate teachers—especially those who would like to explore new technology in their classroom but are intimidated and don't know where to start. I think it is a wonderful place to experiment with web-based technologies in a safe and welcoming space. This is such a great way to encourage and recognize the digital achievement of the staff." (Fleming, 2015a).

This message, among the others, confirmed for her what she already knew—that teachers want to create their own professional learning paths, they want to learn anytime and anywhere, and they want to receive appropriate and authoritative credit for their informal learning. Ms. Fleming believes that the success of this platform rests on the fact that educators can take control of their own learning and that they can therefore learn what they want to learn when they want to learn it.

Educators are happy to have a system that acknowledges their informal learning and appreciate that it is a safe place and not one intended to be used as a formal evaluation tool. Participants are free to learn, experiment, and take risks. Educators everywhere can benefit greatly from this sustained initiative because of the professional learning flexibility an online platform provides. They also benefit from having a means to document the skills they have gained and showcase the learning they have put into practice in the classroom. The success of this sustained initiative has shown that digital badges are evolving into a key credentialing and assessment tool for our times.

DIGITAL BADGING TO SUPPORT STUDENT LEARNING

Digital badges and micro-credentials also can be used as a means to showcase what students have learned. Each digital badge equates to a visual representation of a skill or achievement a student earns when mastering concepts related to the standards being addressed. The badging concept has been used traditionally by the Boy and Girl Scouts for years. Unlike a Scouting badge, which is permanently affixed to a sash or vest, a digital badge exists in cyberspace. Badges earned from multiple institutions can be ported to a central virtual gateway and from there embedded in social media profiles, blogs, and electronic portfolios. This gateway, named a "badging backpack" by Mozilla, serves as a new kind of resume or portfolio (Fontichiaro & Elkordy, 2015).

It is important to make sure that each badge aligns to how each student has constructed new knowledge, acquired and then applied an essential skill, or created a learning artifact. These learning outcomes also should be aligned to the standards being addressed. Fontichiaro and Elkordy (2015) provide key elements when creating digital badges to acknowledge student learning:

- **Learning Objectives.** Each badge should have an objective or outcome that corresponds to what the student has learned or can now demonstrate. These can be aligned to both Common Core and state standards or even a specific skill embedded in these.
- **Performance Task or Required Evidence of Learning.** How did the student demonstrate conceptual mastery (task, project, or other assessment)?
- **Levels-Related Badges.** These can serve as building blocks to deeper learning and more rigorous tasks. Just like in video games, once a basic badge is earned, it can lead to more difficult tasks where more badges are awarded when completed.

Chimacum Middle School (Chimacum, Washington) science teacher Alfonso Gonzalez found that moving to a 1:1 classroom in science with iPads, netbooks, and iMac desktop computers allowed for students to submit work electronically. He noticed that his students still used their paper notebooks, but with access to a device each student also had the option to type his or her work. More and more assignments were able to be completed digitally with more than just text. Student work could include multimedia such as audio, video, animations, digital drawings, and so on. Mr. Gonzalez then made the move to gamification, which included a few changes in how instruction and assessment were introduced to students. Assignments, activities, and labs were seen as quests to be completed:

> Instead of starting with 100 percent and chipping away at it by making mistakes, students started with zero points, called Experience Points or XP. By successfully completing work they earned more and more XP. What a great way to look at it, the more you learn, the more experience you get! (Gonzalez, personal communication, 2015)

This meant that even if it took a student five tries to learn a new concept and demonstrate understanding, that student could still earn the full XP instead of being penalized for making mistakes along the way. Just as in a video game, trying over and over until the level is beaten earns full XP!

Students began as Level 1, and the more XP they gained, the higher levels they attained in class. Leveling up and gaining experience showed students how they were doing in Mr. Gonzalez's class tangibly, but there was another way to show what students were learning or mastering in a gamified classroom. This is when he began to explore the concept of using digital badges as an acknowledgment of skill and concept attainment. He believed that digital badges could serve as evidence of learning in a gamified classroom in addition to XP and levels.

Mr. Gonzalez provides the following explanation:

> Take a unit we do here in the sixth grade on energy transfers. The unit begins with a formative assessment to access students' prior knowledge about energy and energy transfers. Completing the activity earns

students a certain amount of XP. Then there is the lab. Completing the lab, collecting data, analyzing the data, and writing a conclusion earns more XP. Answering follow-up reflection questions earns more XP. Finally, students are asked to apply their knowledge by drawing some energy transfer diagrams, earning the last XP of the unit. By completing all four parts of the unit, the prior knowledge formative assessment, the lab, the reflection, and the application diagrams, students earn the Energy Transfer Badge. The Energy Transfer Badge in this class shows which students successfully completed all four parts of the lesson. The Energy Transfer Badge is evidence of learning the concepts of that specific unit. (Gonzalez, 2015)

Mr. Gonzalez believes that in a 1:1 classroom, teachers will benefit from using a Learning Management System (LMS) such as Moodle to present a unit to students and to keep track of student work using digital badges. As students submit some of their work electronically and some of their work through their notebooks, the teacher can check off who has completed all four parts to know who has earned an Energy Transfer Badge. This can be a lot of work for the teacher, especially if the teacher sees 80 to 140 students a day, as is the case in many secondary schools. Having students report when they have earned a badge as a form of self-assessment can remedy that situation. One problem with having students self-report is that those students who aren't interested in badges will not report when they have earned one. "While that is perfectly OK because not everyone will be interested in getting badges, those students will miss out on the self-assessment component" (Gonzalez, 2015). The key then is for the teacher to develop another means for students to self-report what he or she has learned.

The Energy Transfer Badge that Mr. Gonzalez created was as simple as a graphic with the caption, *Energy Transfer Badge*. One method he tried for giving students their digital badges was to have them copy and paste the image code for the badge, including the caption title, to their blogs. He had a page on his class Moodle with the code for each badge, and students had to copy the code for each badge they earned. There were students who did that successfully—they completed all four parts of the unit, reported to him that they earned the badge, then copied and pasted the badge image code onto their blogs. Some students who completed all four parts of the unit didn't bother to report that they had earned the badge because they didn't want or need the badge to prove they learned the material. Yet some students who reported having earned the badge never got around to copying the badge code to their blogs to display the badge. They reported that it was too difficult to copy and paste the code to their blogs to display the badge. So as easy as it seemed to have students self-report having earned a badge and copy and paste an image code to their blogs to display their badge, it didn't work for everyone. To gamify a course and use badges as evidence of student learning Mr. Gonzalez recommends an LMS that automates the delivery of badges to students, so neither the teacher nor the student has to worry about getting a badge.

One such LMS that Mr. Gonzalez recommends is 3D GameLab (http://www.3dgamelab.com). On 3D GameLab the teacher sets up all assignments, activities, labs, and projects onto the 3D GameLab system. Those assignments, activities, labs, and projects become quests in the 3D GameLab system. One part of the 3D GameLab system is the ability to create badges and assign them to different quests. In the example here, the teacher would assign the prior knowledge formative assessment, the lab, the reflection, and the application diagrams to the Energy Transfer Badge. Once the teacher assigns the quests to a certain badge, 3D GameLab does the rest. As students submit their quests, the teacher approves them if they are done completely or returns the quest to each student with individual feedback on how to complete it successfully. Once students complete all four quests, 3D GameLab automatically assigns the students their XP and the badge! To learn more about how this looks, visit Mr. Gonzalez's blog at http://educatoral.com/ScienceProgress.html (scroll a bit to see the badges section).

From the student's point of view, he or she can click on the badges section of his or her 3D GameLab account and see all the badges he or she has earned! Clicking on any badge shows what assignments, activities, labs, or projects are needed to complete to earn that badge. This includes a quest where students search through all the badges in the course to look for which badges they want to earn while allowing them to set goals. "Including a quest for self-assessment will also ensure that even students who aren't motivated by or interested in badges will still assess their learning in class. There's no limit to what teachers can do with 3D GameLab" (Gonzalez, 2015).

Badges have great potential, and 3D GameLab is working on providing that by allowing badges to be exported to Mozilla Open Badges (http://www.openbadges.org), a resource referenced by Laura Fleming earlier in this chapter. As with many online services, they work better for kids over age 13 because of privacy and online child protection issues. Mr. Gonzalez believes digital badges should go beyond being a picture showing what students have completed. Clicking on a badge should display data about what the holder of the badge has done or can do, what he or she has learned, and so on. Work is being done to move from paper certificates to digital badges, so having students earn digital badges in their K–12 classes will prepare them for using badges in résumés, especially digital résumés.

IMPLEMENTATION TIPS

- Develop a procedure for awarding digital badges aligned to specific criteria, skills, concepts, or standards.
- Decide on a platform (i.e., Mozilla Open Badges), and ensure there is uniformity across the school or district.

- Issue badges when criteria are met.
- Provide the means to display badges using tools such as Credly (for use with educators and students 12 and older). For students under age 12, digital portfolios can be created to house the badges.

SUMMARY

Uncommon learning calls for new ways to provide acknowledgment of learning for both adults and students. Digital badges represent a bold approach to provide evidence of acquired skills and conceptual mastery in a way that is much more meaningful. With traditional professional development and grading, both systems are designed based on rewards in the form of numbers. In the case of professional development, this is typically quantified by hours and, for grades, either letters or percentages. In each case it is often difficult to determine what skills have actually been applied and mastered. Digital badging holds great promise to provide evidence as to what the earner actually knows and can do. The badge in itself signifies a special accomplishment to the earner, which can be proudly shared through a variety of ways.

Academies and Smaller Learning Communities

A True Preparation for College and Careers

Several years ago, a Neptune High School (NHS) student seeking guidance with his college selection approached Principal Richard Allen. The student wanted to identify the best engineering schools he could attend based on his SAT scores and grade point average (GPA). Mr. Allen asked him to be specific about the field of study that interested him. His reply was simply, or naively, "engineering" (Allen, personal communication, 2015). It seemed to Mr. Allen that because of the student's lack of exposure to the professional field of engineering, what he knew was a simplistic summary of the little he had been exposed to in his schooling and by his natural curiosity. The student's lack of exposure was a call to arms for Mr. Allen as a school leader: students needed to be better prepared for college and career, and that required providing students with a curriculum that was based on theory and hands-on learning, *with the emphasis on hands-on experiences.*

The paradigm for career programs Mr. Allen was familiar with came in the form of vocational programs or the narrowly designed academic learning centers found in many schools throughout New Jersey. Each has its merits and its weaknesses. "I envisioned a program that supplemented the students' regular course of study and that did not disaggregate the students from their peers during the school day" (Allen, 2015). This was the genesis of the *JumpStart* Academies of Neptune High School. To date, there are eight such academies: *Communications, Education, Engineering, Environmental Science, Law/Criminal Justice, Medical Science, New Jersey Reserve Officers' Training Corps (NJROTC), and Performing Arts.* Each academy is facilitated by a coordinator whose primary responsibility is to arrange mentoring opportunities, schedule and plan field experiences, and ensure that students fulfill course requirements for graduation.

Students in the NHS *JumpStart* Academies are enrolled in the program of choice after the application process is completed. The application process is a formality to assess the students' interest and desire to participate in the academy of choice. With few exceptions, students are accepted to the program. It is not the mission of the academies to deny any student a chance to participate as a member. This open enrollment philosophy is used as a motivating tool with the hope that the work in the academy will inspire and motivate students to improve their academic skills.

The academies at NHS are rooted in strong academic courses of study with specific course requirements, including advanced placement studies in the students' junior and senior year. In addition, academy students take college-level courses in their fields of study, funded by NHS and the Neptune

Township School District. But at the heart of the program are the mandatory learning experiences that are scheduled before, during, or after school. Students, from time to time, miss other academic classes to attend lectures, field experiences, or mentoring opportunities during the school day. Students are required to meet with their teachers to schedule make-up work and are expected to fulfill their class requirements in a timely manner. This covenant between teacher and students has been very successful (Allen, 2015).

Each academy's success is driven by the partnerships established between the *JumpStart* Academy coordinators and local institutions. Academies have strong partnerships with local government agencies, colleges and universities, hospitals, performing arts centers, and law enforcement agencies. These partnerships are memorialized through memorandums of agreement that outline specific roles for the institutions and the *JumpStart* Academies. The partnerships are renewed every year, with appointed members from each organization or institution acting as equal partners in the planning phase of the curriculum, field experiences, and mentoring aspects of their respective academies.

Though the experience Mr. Allen had with the hopeful engineering student led to the start of the *JumpStart* Academy concept, *JumpStart* Medical Science Academy was born from a need to expose students to medical career fields. *JumpStart* Medical Science grew quickly and naturally with a major teaching hospital in NHS's backyard. The location was not only convenient: it was serendipitous.

As the academy program grew, it became apparent to Mr. Allen that students thrived on the hands-on experiences, mentors became attached to the students who demonstrate a drive, and the academic growth witnessed by the students was indeed fueled by the purposefulness of the curriculum and the engagement students now had with the curriculum. No longer were they taking calculus; they were taking "calculus for medicine." No longer were they taking world history; they were taking "world history for engineers." The curriculum no longer defined the actions of the students; *the students defined their relationships with curriculum.*

"With the inception of the *JumpStart* Academies came the need for us to not only promote but to instantly identify the members of each academy" (Allen, 2015). Without much discussion, it was unanimously agreed upon that every academy member would wear a uniform that identified their academy affiliation. The terms and conditions were clear. When students are working with the academy, they are to wear their uniforms. During the six-hour forensics investigation lectures and mock crime scene investigation, Law/Criminal Justice Academy students were required to wear their uniform, cap, and jacket. Medical Science Academy students wear their lab coats for all hospital rounds, differential diagnosis seminars, and mentoring and volunteering experiences. Scrubs are required for all lab work. Communications Academy students wear their shirts and (*if weather calls for it*) jackets when filming or touring local radio and TV stations and during all mentoring and volunteering experiences. The *JumpStart* Education students wear their sharp, blue-collared, long-sleeve shirts with ties when presenting in front of a class of elementary school students or at various seminars. The signature uniforms identify each academy student, and every academy student wears it proudly.

The *JumpStart* Academy has evolved over the years. It was agreed upon early in the process that the academy structure would be flexible and fluid so that the needs and interests of the students would dictate the curriculum and the various experiences. The coordinators are always reminded that the growth model of the program is limited only by the imagination of the academy coordinator and the mentor–mentee relationships forged. Grades for field experiences are assigned based on competency and participation, but *course or classroom grades are earned in a traditional manner.*

The 2006-to-2007 school year had little in comparison to the 2013-to-2014 school year. The *JumpStart* initiative, along with expanding advanced placement, NHS's dual enrollment program, and the birth of the Early College High School have played a significant role in changing the academic climate and culture of NHS. While many of the class offerings remain static, the *JumpStart* Academy program has piqued the interest of the students and has expanded the walls of the traditional high school setting. Its real-world, authentic, and live event learning model has transformed traditional high school learning into an interactive learning model that places the learner in real world, in real time, with authentic learning and growing experiences (Allen, 2015).

The academies that Richard Allen helped to establish at NHS in New Jersey are what I consider a gold standard in terms of what these programs should look like and how they should function. The entire premise of this initiative is to provide students deeper learner pathways related to college and career interests. We also created our own academies during my tenure as a high school principal. The academies at New Milford High School (NMHS) represented a bold new direction for education in the New Milford Public School District, one that considered student interest, national need, and global demand for highly qualified graduates capable of competing at the most challenging levels (Sheninger, 2014). They debuted in September 2011 and included the Academy of Arts & Letters, the STEM Academy, and the Academy for Global Leadership. Each offered concentrated studies in well-defined, career-focused areas directly connected to university majors and workforce need. The academies at NMHS cultivated emerging professionals who exhibited the knowledge, skill, character, and work ethic necessary for success in the global marketplace (Sheninger, 2014). Junior academies were also developed and implemented at David E. Owens Middle School in New Milford, New Jersey.

CORNERSTONES OF THE ACADEMIES AT NMHS

In addition to the array of career-focused curricula associated with each of the academies, there were special features that further defined the academy experience (Sheninger, 2014):

- Professional mentorships
- Opportunities for dual credit
- Access to resources outside the school setting such as field trips and virtual courses
- Relationships with partnering institutions and organizations, such as the Bergen Performing Arts Center, Rutgers University, St. Thomas Aquinas College, and Farleigh Dickinson University
- Master classes, workshops, and other related field studies
- Book studies
- A capstone project
- Specialized transcripts
- A special designation on a diploma

A specialized endorsement was also available for students to pursue. The Education Endorsement was available for students in all academies. Teachers have the unique ability to promote opportunity for all children and make a lasting impact, now and into the future. Each of the three academies embraced a lifelong passion for learning along with the possibility for future careers in education and offered opportunities to inspire the teachers and caregivers of tomorrow through an Education Endorsement. To nurture many students' interest in teaching as a profession, students in any of the academies were able to take a minimum of two courses, including an elective called of Tomorrow's Teachers, to qualify for the Education Endorsement. Other courses included early childhood development, sociology, psychology, approved virtual high school offerings, and independent study. Academy students also received a special designation upon graduating. Upon successful completion of 50 credits in an academy sequence over a four-year period, students received special academy designation on their high school diplomas. The typical academy student graduates with 130 to 140 credits, which is 10 to 20 more than the New Jersey state requirement for graduation.

In the successful academies at NMHS, students demonstrated an interest and aptitude in a given career-focused area, exhibited evidence of a sound work ethic, possessed a record of exemplary conduct and attendance, and expressed a willingness to immerse oneself in a concentrated course of study over a four-year period. This uncommon learning experience was inclusive of all students regardless of GPA. The premise behind this decision was the belief that all students should be afforded the opportunity to follow their learning passion in a more rigorous and relevant fashion.

Admissions to the academies at NMHS are open to all New Milford students. Applicants are required to submit a statement of interest signed by the student and the student's parents. Applicants also are required to submit with their application an essay describing why enrollment in one of the academies is important to them, what attributes they possess that would contribute positively and productively to the academy community, what they have done personally or through school that illustrated their interest, and what they expect to gain from the academy experience. Applicants also are asked to provide a reference from one of their current teachers endorsing their applications.

Studies in the humanities are interdisciplinary and include courses in literature, cultural studies, history, and the arts. The study of humanities may lead to answers to complex questions, such as how does the past influence the present and the future? Does life imitate art? Why do some titles, essays, speeches, characters, songs, films, plays, and performers endure time, whereas others do not? A student in the Academy of Arts & Letters is not just one who completes a series of liberal arts courses but one who investigates, through critical analysis, and finds value in differing interpretations, perspectives, cultures, and opinions.

There are two concentrations within the program, humanities and performing arts. A humanities concentration prepares students for professions in many fields including but not limited to: law, diplomacy, politics, journalism, education, literature, psychology, activism, environmentalism, and broadcasting. The performing arts concentration appeals to students who demonstrate talents and passions for the performing arts, including opportunities for the performer to use his or her own body, face, and voice or use musical instruments, clay, metal, paint, and technology for exploration and creative expression.

Students interested in the Academy of Arts and Letters possess the desire to create, question, respond, critique, and communicate with others in writing, in speaking, and through works of art. The program encourages self-reflection, which in turn helps develop personal consciousness, often combined with an active sense of civic duty. As a capstone experience, it is encouraged that students reach out across disciplines and cultures to deepen their understanding of a work of literature, a time period in history, a figure in history or art, a genre, or an artistic milieu through independent or work related study, internship, or travel.

Studies in the Academy for Global Leadership (AGL) are interdisciplinary and include a variety of core and elective courses in business, international affairs, world languages, humanitarian studies, global perspectives in literature, and ethics. Students within the AGL have the option for a business concentration through participation in a project-based course of studies. The goal of the AGL is to prepare a new generation of critical thinkers for effective and ethical leadership, ready to act as global citizens in addressing international and national issues across cultures. Study in AGL may lead a student to answers to complex questions, such as what is the role of the United States in world diplomacy and the ethical treatment of human beings? How do we promote ethical business practices nationally and internationally? Are we within our rights to impose American values of democracy and capitalism on other nations?

Students in AGL complete a series of core and elective courses, cultivating written and oral communication skills, interpersonal skills, problem solving, diplomacy, multicultural sensitivity, tolerance, acceptance, and the differences between critical and normative thinking. There is an emphasis on research, international study, and debate. Value is placed on both individual progress and collaborative efforts as students are exposed to the rigors and challenges of a diverse, interdependent world. Course work is designed to allow students to identify, cultivate, and assert their leadership qualities in preparation for professions in many fields including but not limited to: international business, foreign affairs, world languages, humanitarian efforts, economics, public speaking, library studies, law, politics, and education.

The program encourages students to think critically and reflectively in the development of multicultural awareness, business acumen, ethical behavior, and active contribution to a global society. As a capstone experience, students are encouraged to reach across disciplines and cultures to exercise their leadership capacity through independent or work-related study, internships, networking, or travel.

Studies in the Science, Technology, Engineering and Mathematics (STEM) Academy are interdisciplinary in nature and include a variety of required courses and electives. STEM fields are collectively considered core technological underpinnings of an advanced society. In many forums, including political, governmental, and academic, the strength of the STEM workforce is viewed as an indicator of a nation's ability to sustain itself. STEM studies may lead to answers to complex questions: What is our place in the universe? How do bioethical issues impact our society? What is the relationship between design and invention to human development? How do STEM disciplines assist us in our ability to compete in a global society?

A student in the STEM Academy is not just one who completes a series of math and science courses but also one who enjoys learning through investigation; scientific, technological, and mathematical inquiry; and discovery and analysis. The STEM Academy prepares students for professions in many fields including but not limited to: psychology, environmental studies, biochemistry, medicine, engineering, accounting, education, architecture, aeronautics, statistics, computer sciences, food sciences, and applied mathematics. Core and elective offerings appeal to students who find themselves drawn to these disciplines. These students possess an innate curiosity to inquire, investigate, problem solve, create, experiment, apply, and reflect on and critique their findings. The goal for STEM students is to cultivate a group of future leaders who possess the ability to think critically as a result of deep analysis. The program encourages the students to engage in self-reflection, which in turn, helps develop solid content knowledge, personal consciousness, ethical behavior, and active contribution to the STEM workforce. As a capstone experience, students are encouraged to reach across disciplines and cultures to deepen their understanding of an area under the STEM umbrella through independent or work-related study, internship, or travel.

The academies initiative made us critically look at our course of studies and what classes we were offering out students. During the initial planning stages we quickly realized that to offer a robust, rigorous program that catered to our students' interests, we had to add a variety of new courses. For student to engage in deeper learning opportunities during the school day, we needed to ensure that each academy tract had a variety of courses aligned to each focus area. The integration of academies compelled us to add 20 new courses over a two-year period. As a small school this posed quite the challenge, as many of these new courses were singletons, which added to the complexity of developing a master schedule. This challenge did not deter us from providing a more relevant learning experience for those students who wished to pursue a more challenging pathway aligned to college and career interests.

Students also feel more relevancy in terms of their learning. Each year academy students are placed in a grade level cohort and engaged in authentic learning opportunities in addition to their selected course work. Outside learning experiences are made available throughout the year aligned to each specific academy. Academy students engage in a specialized project during each of the four marking periods, which allows them to apply concepts mastered during their course work. These projects are intimately connected to their learning interests and academy designation. Upon graduation, each academy cohort wears medals with a unique crest that their peers designed during the first year of the academies. Each medal is connected to a ribbon that has specific colors associated with each academy. There is also a special designation in the graduation program that identifies which academy each student is graduating from. All of these little perks help acknowledge the learning efforts of our students.

SMALLER LEARNING COMMUNITIES

For many years New Dorp High School did not have the best reputation among public schools on Staten Island. The school was plagued with an array of challenges such as poor attendance, below-average achievement, and low graduation rates. According to Deirdre DeAngelis, who took over the principalship in 1999, parent support for what the school could offer prospective students was dismal. Since her arrival things have changed dramatically. Graduation and attendance rates have drastically increased. The school even has been recognized nationally as a model for education reform (Tyre, 2012). Families are now choosing to send their children to New Dorp High School as part of New York City's open enrollment process, through which parents can apply to send their children to any public school in the five boroughs.

Part of the transformation efforts came in 2005. Even though progress had been made since 1999, New Dorp was still struggling and consistently failed to make adequate yearly progress as defined by No Child Left Behind (NCLB). There was a pressing need to change the culture of the building, and as a result Deirdre DeAngelis applied for a series of grants. A significant turning point came when the school received one particular grant from the Bill & Melinda Gates Foundation to transform the large, urban school into a system of eight smaller learning communities (SLCs).

Approximately 10 years later, the school now gets flooded with calls from parents requesting spots for their children in one of eight tailored learning programs, or communities, that New Dorp High School now offers. The SLCs are organized around different curricular themes and function like schools-within-a-school, where teachers and students select a program based on their interest. These smaller programs provide students with more personalized learning experiences, where teachers and counselors develop more meaningful relationships with a smaller number of students. This reorganization was meant to address some of the structural challenges common among large, high-need urban schools by establishing more personalized learning environments for all students.

As a comprehensive high school, New Dorp now provides a small, personalized setting for each student in one of the theme-based or career-focused SLCs. A challenging learning environment, rich in instructional techniques and support services, combined with a large variety of extracurricular activities, prepares students for college and career opportunities. All students, grades 9 through 12, are enrolled in one of the following eight SLCs:

- Future Teachers Academy. A high school teacher preparatory program that includes courses in child development, psychology, children's literature, teaching methodology, as well as a college-credited education course. A student teaching component is required.
- Law Institute and Air Force JROTC. A Gilder Lehrman Institute of American History–sponsored program that focuses on electives in law, history, and human rights. Also includes the award-winning Virtual Enterprise Law program. Students visit historic sites such as

Philadelphia, Gettysburg, and Washington, DC. These exciting trips support and enhance classroom instruction. The law program also instituted the JROTC Air Force Program in September 2013.

- **Corporate Center for Business & Technology—Career and Technical Education (CTE).** Combines technology, business, and academics with real-world learning experiences. Includes preparation for MS Office Specialist Certification, the award-winning Virtual Enterprise Program, and college courses.
- **Mathematics & Science Institute.** A competitive program that prepares students for college majors that lead to careers as physicians, dentists, pharmacists, and biochemical engineers. College-level courses, internships, and SAT/ACT preparation are required.
- **Academy of Communication & Media Arts.** Utilizing hands-on experiences, students will explore all facets of media arts, including TV, film, the Internet, radio, and print media. The emphasis is on exposing students to career and postsecondary opportunities in this field.
- **Academy of Fine & Dramatic Arts.** Program dedicated to nurturing artistically talented students while providing comprehensive regents-level instruction. Affords students the opportunity to pursue and develop their artistic interests through course work, showcases, and performances.
- **Institute of Health Sciences & Culinary Arts.** An academically rigorous program that will prepare students for college as well as careers in the health care profession. Some of the potential careers include physicians, nurses, athletic trainers, physical and occupational therapists, medical technologists, and medical assistants. The students receive hands-on experience at a local physical therapy facility, where they work alongside physical therapists in creating rehabilitation plans for patients. Students who choose the Culinary Program

will participate in electives that will prepare them for culinary competitions as well as careers in the culinary arts.

- **Institute of Forensic Science & Criminology.** Focuses on real-world applications of forensic science, and incorporates this theme into all subject areas. Students will be exposed to criminalistics through field trips, guest speakers, hands-on learning, and discovery-based course work.

Additional branches of the SLCs include the Software Engineering program and the Air Force JROTC program. Students are exposed to real-world career experiences: for example, the Future Teachers Academy has a student teaching component; the media students have an online newspaper and a weekly newscast; the Law Institute has internships and mock trial and moot court competitions; and the Health Science students shadow physical therapists and athletic trainers.

The special qualities of these SLCs include the following:

- Students choose a program based on their interest during the admissions and articulation process.
- Students take the majority of their classes in the same wing; therefore, student traffic throughout the building is minimized.
- Teachers choose programs in a manner similar to students and remain dedicated to that program and its students.
- An assistant principal and a team of two teacher coordinators supervise each program. This allows for more direct supervision of a smaller number of students.
- Each program has its own guidance counselor and the assistance of a dedicated school aide who is responsible for outreach to parents regarding attendance and cutting.
- There are no more than 400 students in each program.
- Curriculum and course sequences are continually updated to incorporate interdisciplinary units as well

as the themes of these programs to enhance instruction and support the needs of all students.

- English language learners (ELLs) and students with special needs are included in the SLC of their choice and receive mandated services as prescribed.
- Students receive the benefits of a large school, such as a comprehensive physical education program, extensive advance placement course offerings, and a large variety of extracurricular activities.

The New Dorp High School community is extremely proud of the consistent improvement in student data. They have seen a steady increase in graduations each year, yielding more than a 23 percent increase since June of 2005. They have set a goal for the class of 2015 to achieve at least an 80 percent graduation rate (DeAngelis, personal communication, 2015). In addition, as indicated on a recent School Quality Guide, New Dorp has experienced further improvements in their "Weighted Regents Pass Rates" in each content area. Credit accumulation data reveal that students here outperform peer group schools by 5 to more than 23 percent, depending on the category and grade level. The school has also seen an increase in attendance rates.

As a school community, New Dorp believes that the secret to success is twofold: a structural and instructional focus. First, the personalized settings of the SLCs allow students to learn in environments that offer courses of study that are of interest to them, provide the same guidance counselor for four years of high school, and allow the dedicated staff to really get to know everything about their students. Nobody slips through the cracks. Second, teachers meet daily to discuss student work, student data, and student outcomes during their much-focused inquiry work. The findings of their inquiry work inform curriculum development, professional development, and instructional practices. Collaborative teacher teams work together to develop strategies, interventions, and practices that not only meet the skill needs of the students but is also rigorous, fun, and relevant. One of their strongest practices is an interdisciplinary writing program: the Judith Hochman Writing Program. Students develop strong writing skills in all content classrooms during their first two years at New Dorp. By the time they are high school juniors, they are ready to begin college-level writing work. "We are confident that this contributes to the fact that we are graduating students that are college and career ready" (DeAngelis, 2015).

The improved student data and successful school reform efforts have led to recognition by the National Center for Learning Disabilities, awarding New Dorp High School with the Pete and Carrie Rozelle Award. The NYC Department of Education recognized New Dorp as both a Learning Partners School and a Showcase School. The Fund for Public Schools awarded the Sloan Award for Mathematics and Science Instruction to one of their teachers, and the College Board recognized New Dorp as a model school. Their students have won national and local essay contests, Law Institute students were finalists in the mock trial competition, and their Virtual Enterprise students have won first place in the regional competition seven out of the last nine years, taken the NYC title five of the last six years, and placed in the top three nationally five out of the last six years. The students participate in internships connected to the themes of their SLCs throughout Staten Island and beyond, and the Health Science students receive direct instruction from licensed physical therapists and athletic trainers. "Our focus is to give students a 'real-life' experience, preparing them for college and career while making their four years of high school relevant and fun" (DeAngelis, 2015).

IMPLEMENTATION TIPS

- Analyze existing course offerings and curriculum to determine the types of academies or SLCs to be implemented.
- Poll students and staff for suggestions on additional courses to be added.

- Determine additional staffing needs for new courses and who will oversee each academy or SLC.
- Develop specific criteria for each unique academy or SLC.
- Create a budget for unique learning experiences that will be a part of each academy or SLC.

SUMMARY

Academy programs and SLCs are uncommon learning options that cater to student interests and passions. These initiatives provide not only more choice but also more rigorous options to make the learning experience more relevant. They can be implemented in a variety of ways, some of which require very little in terms of financial resources. In the end they afford learners the option to engage in course work and authentic learning experiences that will better prepare them for college and career success. If this is ultimately the goal of schools, then we must critically look at how our schools are structured and function.

Connected Learning

During my first couple of years as principal, I was in a rut and didn't know it. I led my school in a way that I was brainwashed into thinking was the only way. Education had become more about schooling than learning. Then it happened. My epiphany came in 2009 when I begrudgingly decided to give Twitter a try to improve communications with my stakeholders. Little did I know that this moment in time would totally redefine my purpose in education. As my behavior shifted from communicator to learner, I immediately discovered how blinded I was by a system so entrenched in methodologies and practices designed for a period in time that had long passed. I learned how to unlearn and then relearn through conversations I began having with passionate educators across the globe. These conversations empowered me to begin the process of taking my school in a better direction for the sake of my students.

My connected colleagues provided daily inspiration, support, feedback, resources, ideas, and strategies that I used to grow as an educator and leader. As my fixed mind-set evolved into one more focused on growth, the seeds for change were planted and began to take root. With a diligent focus on modeling, changes to school culture slowly began to be embraced by teachers and students alike. This was not an easy journey. During the beginning years I felt more isolated from my colleagues across my district and state than ever before. They did not see nor care to hear about the inherent value in connected learning. Excuses often followed as a bunker mentality overshadowed the potential value that lay in using social media to become a better leader and learner. The only thing that kept me going was that once I had experienced the value for myself, there was no turning back.

At this point I feel the results speak for themselves. New Milford High School (NMHS) became a globally recognized model for what is possible in education during my tenure as principal, and it all started when I became connected. After that my role in the transformation process was placing my teachers and students in a position to experience the value for them. Change became a collaborative and collective process that resulted in a school more focused on learning and one that worked better for kids than adults. With all the challenges brought about by current education reform efforts, we moved forward with a bold vision for growth and innovation. Even though learning across all spectrums looked different, achievement rose in virtually every area. More importantly though was the fact that students appreciated the changes. Had I not become connected, I can say with certainty that my school would not have changed.

Personal Learning Networks

At the heart of a connected model of learning is the concept of a personal learning network (PLN). The concept of a PLN has been around for a very long time. PLNs back in the day consisted of individuals with the same professional interests engaging in mostly face-to-face communication. Fast forward a good amount of years, and enter the Internet. No one can argue that the evolution of the real-time web has dramatically altered how we communicate, gather information, and reflect. The construction of a PLN enables educators to harness the power inherent in 21st-century technologies to create a professional growth tool that is accessible whenever, wherever. In particular, a PLN can provide any educator with a constant supply of resources, thought-provoking discussions, knowledge, leadership strategies, and ways to successfully integrate technology. An educator's PLN provides the fuel for uncommon learning both in and out of the classroom.

The power of connected learning is that we become the epicenter of our learning and determine what, where, and when we want to learn. This makes the learning process meaningful, relevant, applicable, and convenient. With these structures in place, the foundation is established to unleash passion, creativity, and a pursuit of innovation to do what we do better. Connectedness and control of our learning provide each of us with the ability to determine our own path and to differentiate to meet each of our diverse learning needs.

This type of learning is fueled by intrinsic motivation, which is the most pivotal ingredient essential to lifelong learning, growth, innovation, and sustainable change. Each connected educator has access to a wealth of free resources. Using tools to share and acquire resources expands our horizons. Many educators, including myself a few years ago, didn't even know these tools existed, let alone how they could enhance the teaching and learning process. A PLN establishes a two-way mechanism for constructive feedback, support, and advice. In my mind this is priceless. No longer do we need to feel like we inhabit isolated islands in our respective positions.

Cost is at times a prohibitive factor to learning, but you do not have to pay for this powerful opportunity to grow. All it costs is an investment of time, which you ultimately determine. This meaningful investment of time will provide you with the ability and means to connect with the best minds in the field of education. One of the most amazing attributes associated with social media is that it makes the world a much smaller place. You can now connect with world-renowned educational researchers or experts from your living room. Possibly even more powerful is the ability to learn from actual practitioners doing the same job as you. Accessibility to these ideas, strategies, and collective knowledge from both of these groups will ultimately make you a better educator. Silos of information become a thing of the past.

Developing a PLN

It is important to understand what tools are available to build a PLN. After all it is the tools that allow for like-minded educators to connect and engage in conversations that have the potential to radically transform professional practice. The following is a quick list of tools that can be used to begin building your own PLN (Sheninger, 2014):

- **Twitter (http://www.twitter.com).** A microblogging platform that allows educators from all corners of the globe to communicate in 140 characters or fewer and allows for the sharing of resources, discussion of best practices, and collaboration.
- **LinkedIn (http://www.linkedin.com).** A professional networking site that allows educators to connect, exchange ideas, and find opportunities. Educators can join a variety of groups that cater to their individual learning interests and engage in discussions as well as submit, read, and comment on articles.
- **Blogs.** Incredible sources of information that allow educators to reflect, share opinions, and discuss various topics. This is a common medium with which to discover best practices, examples of innovation, and professional experiences of both novice and veteran educators. Common blogging applications include

Blogger (http://www.blogger.com), WordPress (http://www.wordpress.org), and TypePad (http://www.typepad.com).

- RSS Readers. A Real Simple Syndication (RSS) reader is a tool that allows leaders to keep up with educational blogs, news, wikis, and podcasts all in one convenient location. By subscribing to various RSS feeds, leaders create a customized flow of information that is continually updated and accessible through the use of mobile devices or the Internet. Leaders can even create their own RSS feeds! Popular RSS readers include Feedly (http://www.feedly.com) and RSSOwl (http://www.rssowl.org).
- Tablet and Smartphone Apps. Free apps for iOS (Apple) and Android devices tap into existing RSS feeds and social networks to create customized sources of educational information. The Flipboard app (http://www.flipboard.com) will tune any leader's social networks and RSS feeds into a digital magazine that can be navigated with the flip of a finger.
- Digital Discussion Forums. Communities of educators interested in similar topics. One of the most popular sites is called Ning, where educators can create or join specific communities. Ning sites offer a range of learning and growth options such as discussion forums, event postings, messaging, news articles, chat features, groups, and videos. Popular educational Ning sites for leaders include the Educator's PLN (http://www.edupln.ning.com) and Classroom 2.0 (http://www.classroom20.com). Some other fantastic digital discussion forums are ASCD Edge (http://ascdedge.ascd.org), which you must be a member of ASCD to use, and edWeb.net.
- Social Bookmarking. A method for storing, organizing, curating, and sharing bookmarks online. There are no better tools out there than social bookmarking tools, which allow busy leaders to make order out of the chaos

that initially emerges with access to the amazing resources made available through PLNs. Social bookmarking tools allow educators to store all of their resources in the cloud, which are then accessible from an Internet-connected device. Popular sites such as Delicious (http://www.delicious.com) and Diigo (http://www.diigo.com) allow leaders to add descriptions as well as categorize each site using tags. Educators can even join groups and receive e-mail updates when new bookmarks are added. Diigo has expanded features that allow users to highlight and annotate the Web sites that they bookmark.

- **Facebook.** A social networking site that allows people not only to keep up with family and friends but also to connect and engage with professionals. Many national and state educational organizations have created Facebook pages as places for leaders to congregate online, engage in conversations on professional practice, and share resources. Each customizable page or group provides a variety of learning opportunities and growth options for educators.

- **Google+.** Within Google+, users can create a profile page similar to Facebook, group people in circles (organize people into categories), and set up free group video chats called hangouts. Each hangout can include up to nine different people from anywhere in the world.

- **Pinterest (http://www.pinterest.com).** The best way to describe this tool is as an electronic bulletin board where users can "pin" images from around the web. For visual learners, it is a great way to curate resources and other information. Images that are pinned are categorized into various user-defined boards on one's profile. Images are linked to Web sites, and pins can be shared and searched for.

- **Voxer (http://www.voxer.com).** Voxer is a simple-to-use push-to-talk app that has been embraced by the education community. With Voxer, educators can participate in private or group voice conversations that are threaded. The functionality of Voxer also allows users to send images and text, including web links.

- **Periscope (https://www.periscope.tv/).** Periscope is a free, live video streaming app for iOS and Android devices. As a live video streaming platform, educators can transmit live recordings of themselves to Periscope and Twitter followers. Because Periscope is owned by Twitter, it automatically links to your Twitter account. Users get a notification anytime the educators you're following do a live transmission. Periscope is great for catching glimpses of live presentations at conferences or sharing knowledge instantly using the power of video. You can re-watch any video from your followers for 24 hours after the live broadcast, but after that they disappear and are not permanently archived.

IMPLEMENTATION TIPS

- Pick one tool mentioned in this chapter for the foundation of your PLN. Once mastered, begin slowly to add others.
- Make time each day to engage in learning activities that are important to you.
- Watch how other educators use the tools to develop your own strategy for use.
- Add and remove both people and tools that comprise your PLN based on their return on your time investment.
- Eventually move from a connected lurker to willing participant and collaborative learner in online spaces with your PLN.

SUMMARY

Your PLN will provide you with the seeds of change, but it is up to you to plant, take care of, and cultivate them to witness their growth and development into transformative culture elements (Sheninger, 2014). If you do, it will not take long before these seeds of change mature and begin to bear fruit by becoming embedded, sustainable components of the school culture and your professional growth. With the tools that are now available, connectedness should be the standard, not just an option in education.

Schools That Work for Students

My son Nicholas is your typical child growing up in the 21st century. He loves to play outside, swim in the pool, golf in the NYC Junior Golf League, have friends over, and feast on McDonald's. Then there is the technology aspect of his life, which is a very big part. Who am I to deprive him access to an array of engaging tools that his generation is growing up with? It would be hard to, even if I tried, as the Sheninger household has 30 connected devices in it. He has his devices, which include access to an iTouch, laptop, Nintendo 3DS, Xbox Kinect, and Wii U. Just like his daddy, my son loves his technology. Even though he plays a variety of games with his friends, by far his most favorite is Minecraft.

On a typical Saturday morning, for example, you would think that there is a playdate going on in our playroom where the Xbox is. You literally hear at times five different little voices. Once you enter the room, though, you see only my son who has connected with his friends in numerous states through the Xbox. Not only are they all engaged, but also they are collaborating, communicating, solving problems, strategizing, and thinking critically to create their own unique world. What I just described in the last sentence are commonly referred to as 21st-century skills (we have called them essential skills at my school for the past three years). However, I believe that these skills are paramount to success in the 21st century and beyond. My son and children around the world need these skills as well as experiential learning opportunities that allow them to follow their passions while unleashing their innate desire to be creative.

Some of the best learning and bonding conversations I have with my son are when he explains his rationale and thinking that have gone into creating various Minecraft worlds. His learning is evident as he meticulously explains the structure and function of the different worlds he has created. One of the best designs I ever saw was a McDonald's that he created. It had the golden arches as well as the color red associated with the company's brand. Now you couldn't order a Big Mac or Happy Meal, but he had it designed in a way that you could grab a turkey to satisfy your hunger. As a parent and educator, seeing his creations, discovering his methodology, and basking in his enthusiasm never gets old. In my opinion, this is learning at its finest, driven by authentic engagement, passion, and creativity.

Here is the major problem though. The structure and function of the majority of schools in this country are the exact opposite of the world that our learners are growing up in. When one looks at education in general, there is very little change from more than 150 years ago. Back then the education system was designed to serve an industrialized world that was in desperate need of skilled factory workers. What resulted was the quick development of a system to educate as many students as possible in a fashion that was cheap and easy. Conforming to this system created masses of compliant students who ultimately acquired the necessary skills to assist society in becoming more industrialized.

Fast-forward 150 years, and you will notice that the world has radically changed, but education has not. What are we really preparing our students for now? There is an automatic disconnect when students like my son, regardless of their grade level, walk into schools with a lack of engagement, relevancy, meaning, and authentic learning opportunities. Our education system has become so efficient in sustaining a century-old model because it is easy and safe. The resulting conformity has resulted in a sterilization of learning among our students as they see so little value in the cookie-cutter learning exercises they are forced to go through each day. The bottom line is that they are bored. It is time that we create schools that work for our students as opposed to ones that have traditionally worked well for the adults.

Creating schools that work for students requires a bold vision for change that not only tackles the status quo inherent in the industrialized model of education but also challenges some current education reform efforts. Yes, there are challenges and pressures associated with many mandates and directives that have been quickly implemented in schools, but they are not insurmountable. Each challenge should not be viewed as an obstacle but as an opportunity to take action and do things differently in a way that will inspire kids to develop a love and appreciation for learning. Uncommon learning options not only accomplish this but also address higher standards in the process.

How you go about implementing uncommon learning initiatives will vary from school to school, but the process begins with the simple notion of putting students first to allow them to follow their passions, create, tinker, invent, play, and collaborate. Schools that work for students focus less on control and more on trust. Most importantly, they are places where kids actually look forward to coming. The time for excuses is over, and taking action is the only logical choice if we are committed to real change. Positive change is happening across the country as evidenced in this book. Now it is up to you to be the change that you wish to see in education.

There is a common fallacy that school administrators are the leaders of change. This makes a great sound bite, but the reality is that many individuals in leadership positions are not actually working directly with students. Teachers are the true catalysts of change that can create schools that work for kids. They are the ones, after all, who are tasked with implementing the myriad directives and mandates that come their way. Leadership is about action, not position. Schools need more teacher leaders who are empowered through autonomy to take calculated risks to develop innovative approaches that enable deeper learning and higher-order thinking without sacrificing accountability. If the goal in fact is to increase these elements in our education system, then we have to allow students to demonstrate learning in a variety of ways.

For change to be successful, it must be sustained. Teacher leaders must not only be willing to see the process through, but they also must create conditions that promote a change in mentality. It really is about moving from a fixed to a growth mind-set, something that many educators and schools are either unwilling or afraid to do. What I have learned is that if someone understands why change is needed and the elements already discussed become an embedded component of school culture, he or she or the system ultimately will experience the value for themselves. The change process then gets a boost from an intrinsic motivational force that not only jump-starts the initiative but allows for the embrace of change as opposed to looking for buy-in. We should never have to "sell" people on better ways to do our noble work nor rely on mandates and directives. These traditional pathways used to drive change typically result in resentment, undermining, and failure. Move uncommon learning initiatives forward in these ways:

- **Building a Shared Vision.** This important aspect is notably absent in many uncommon leaning initiatives. Efforts must be made to develop a shared vision with a variety of stakeholders, including students. This is vital if the goal is a sustained, cross-curricular application on a routine basis. The vision should be established in a way that clearly articulates how the uncommon learning initiative will be used to support and enhance student learning.

- **Developing a Strategic Plan Backed by Action.** Begin to form a plan for uncommon learning using essential questions that add perspective for the change: Why is this change needed? How will it be implemented? What resources are needed? How will we monitor progress and evaluate on a consistent basis? What other challenges have to be overcome? How will it impact our students? Refer to the strategies in Chapter 2 to address these important questions, while the subsequent chapters illustrate how they can guide you on a journey to implement uncommon learning initiatives successfully in your school or district. These questions and others combined with practitioner examples will help you develop a concrete plan for action.

- **Understanding That Access Matters.** During the planning process it is imperative that there is a critical analysis of existing infrastructure. There is nothing more frustrating to teachers and students than when an activity incorporating technology fails because of poor Wi-Fi connectivity. In addition to Wi-Fi, it is important to ensure that there are enough devices and associated software if the goal is integration across the curriculum. To increase access give some thought to a bring your own device (BYOD) initiative if there is not enough funding to go 1:1. An audit of available resources during the planning process would be a wise idea.

- **Ensure Ongoing Professional Learning.** I cannot overstate the importance of this suggestion enough. Teachers need training on how to develop pedagogically sound lessons and quality assessments aligned to higher standards. They also need to be exposed to a variety of tools and ways that they can be seamlessly integrated to support specified learning outcomes. School leaders need professional learning opportunities that assist them to observe and evaluate digital learning effectively in classrooms. Professional learning should be ongoing and embedded throughout the school year.

- **Monitoring With Intent.** The vision and planning process provides the focus, but consistent monitoring helps to ensure sustainable change leading to transformation. School leaders need to consistently monitor and provide feedback on uncommon learning activities through observations, evaluations, walk-throughs, and collecting artifacts.

- **Providing Support.** Throughout the initial implementation stages, and well after the initiative gains steam, ongoing support needs to be provided. Support comes in many ways, such as empowering teachers to be innovative through autonomy, giving up control, being flexible, and encouraging risk taking. Budget allocations will also have to be made each year not only to sustain current digital learning initiatives but also to move forward.

- **Modeling the Way.** To put it simply, don't expect others to do what you will not. Attempt to model at a basic level the expectations that you have when it comes to digital learning. Don't be afraid to roll up your sleeves and work alongside your colleagues.

- **Honoring Student Voice and Choice.** Uncommon learning initiatives are all about creating schools that work for students. When developing lessons allow students to decide which digital tools they want to use to show you what they have learned. The key is being able to assess learning, not knowing how to use thousands of tools. Put students in the driver's seat when it comes to allowing them to determine the right tool for the right task. Also encourage them to consistently provide input to improve uncommon learning initiatives.

A TEACHER–LEADER IN ACTION:
THE EPIC *ROMEO AND JULIET* PROJECT

Romeo and Juliet had always been a tough sell for Nick Provenzano's students, an English teacher at Grosse Pointe South High School in Grosse Pointe Farms, Michigan. "Teaching a play, any play, is tough because they are not meant to be read. They are meant to be performed" (Provenzano, personal communication, 2015). He was really torn in what to do because *Romeo and Juliet* is a wonderful play that he wanted his students to love and appreciate as much as he did. This is when Mr. Provenzano decided that the best way to make that happen was to do exactly what Shakespeare wanted: have the students perform.

Mr. Provenzano was never one to take the easy road when it came to projects. "Go big or go home has always been part of my lesson planning" (Provenzano, 2015). Just performing in class would not be enough to get the students motivated. Thus he looked for a way to turn it up a notch, and Van Meter, Iowa, was the perfect school to help with that. With the help of Shannon Miller, the librarian for Van Meter, she connected Mr. Provenzano with their freshmen English teacher, Shawn Hyer. Together they came up with a plan to have their students work together all year on various projects. They did literature circles and connected after reading other stories. They used wikis and blogs to communicate. "We built the collaboration aspects of the *Romeo and Juliet* project before we started this big project. We needed a firm foundation if we were going to ask the students to engage in a project that has never been done before" (Provenzano, 2015).

The Epic *Romeo and Juliet* Project had students from two different schools put on a version of the play. Despite being separated by hundreds of miles and a time zone, students were given the chance to create a version of *Romeo and Juliet* that they wanted to see. Students chose various parts in the project (writers, directors, actors, advertising, music, etc.) and went to work. The writers decided to update the play, set it in modern times, and have it revolve around two rival private schools. Students connected using social media and Skype to make sure that everything was going according to plan. In the end, students created a 90-minute version of *Romeo and Juliet* and held a joint premiere on a Saturday afternoon (Provenzano, 2015).

Students were immersed in Shakespeare in a way that Mr. Provenzano had never seen. "They researched the language, studied period costumes, looked into fair-use music, and made their lives all about *Romeo and Juliet* in a way that I have never seen before" (Provenzano, 2015). The students loved the play because they were allowed to explore it on their own terms. They spent hours on their own time learning all about the popular play and commented that this was the best lesson they had all year. These students talked about this project and how much they learned for years. "When I look back at the project, I see students who were engaged in learning in a way that a worksheet or a quiz could never assess" (Provenzano, 2015)—an uncommon learning project indeed.

Teachers should no longer be forced to prepare students for a world that no longer exists and be held accountable through one-dimensional means. Teacher success should be judged on the products students create with real-world tools to solve real-world problems. If teaches are allowed to innovate and allow students to create artifacts of learning to demonstrate conceptual mastery, the end goal should be the acquisition of higher-order thinking skills. This is the heart of uncommon learning, and the result is creating schools that work for our students.

Appendix A

Collaboration Across the Curriculum to Support Common Core

Name _____ Period _____

Date _____ Due Date _____

DIET ANALYSIS: AN INFOGRAPHIC PROJECT

Directions: For this assignment you will present the data you collected in your food log graphically. You must include <u>four</u> components:

1. Either a <u>bar graph, a column graph, a pie chart, or a hierarchy</u> infographic that presents the percentage of each type of food consumed in the individual's overall diet.

*You must have a title for your infographic, along with accurate data and creative and thoughtful use of color.

2. <u>A paired infographic</u> that presents the recommended daily allowances of each food group.

3. <u>An analysis paragraph</u> that specifically explains how the individual's diet compares to the recommended diet, specifically stating which food groups present a problem for the individual, listing and describing the <u>five</u> most serious conditions and diseases that person is at risk for because they eat too much or too little of certain nutrients, and presenting conclusions and recommendations for specific changes that must be made in the individual's diet to improve long-term health.

4. A <u>Works Cited page</u> that lists the sources you used for your graphics and data.

Analysis of Data and Presentation of Analysis: 72 percent

Requirement Checklist: 28 percent

_____ */6 Title for each infographic*

_____ */12 All food groups presented*

_____ */10 Clarity and use of color*

Category	4	3	2	1
Comparison	The comparison is the thorough and complete. Addresses how or why the two diets compare/differ.	The comparison is somewhat thorough. Some gaps appear or there are inconsistencies.	There are glaring omissions in the meaning of the data.	No comparison has been made.
Conditions and Diseases	A minimum of five conditions are listed AND thoroughly described. All information is accurate and reasoning is provided for the selection of each condition.	3-4 conditions are listed OR the discussion is less thorough than a 4. OR there are few inaccuracies—OR the reasoning is lacking in some way.	Only 1-2 conditions are listed. The discussion is sparse OR very inaccurate. OR the student only presents the data and provides no analysis or rationale regarding its importance.	Conditions are merely listed OR so few that the student demonstrates no awareness of the relationship between health and diet.
Conclusions/ Recommendations	Student makes an accurate and well-reasoned conclusion regarding specific changes that must occur. (Go beyond the data to consider lifestyle changes.)	Student makes an accurate but less insightful conclusion regarding specific changes that must occur.	Student has some accuracies in their conclusion—but the overall feeling is that data are merely restated and no real thought is demonstrated.	Conclusions are not attempted.

Appendix B

Essential Skill Sets

- **Creativity.** Web 2.0 tools, social media, and mobile learning devices have the power to unleash the creativity of our students. Adobe also is a worldwide leader in providing a host of tools that can unleash creativity in our students. They not only allow students to demonstrate conceptual mastery through learning artifacts but allow them to create their own form of art. By doing so, a culture of learning is established that will make our students indispensable as they move onward into college and careers.
- **Collaboration.** Digital tools allow students to collaborate on projects and other activities regardless of time and location. This skill provides a competitive advantage to students as they no longer have to rely on strictly meeting face-to-face to complete learning tasks together. More and more career paths rely on teamwork to complete projects through the use of technology.
- **Communication.** Effective communication is one of the most important skills needed to succeed in today's society. Digital tools expose students to a variety of means to communicate in the real world through social networks, Web 2.0 tools, and video conferencing.

- **Critical Thinking and Problem Solving.** Digital tools provide learners with the media to reason effectively through both induction and deduction, use systems thinking, solve problems in innovative ways, and make judgments and decisions through analysis, reflection, synthesis, and evaluation. They also can be used to solve complete problems and develop unique solutions that traditional means cannot.
- **Entrepreneurism.** An often overlooked or undervalued skill, entrepreneurism can be developed and enhanced through the use of digital tools to solve problems and create artifacts of learning. It instills a sense of taking risks and dealing with failure along the road to success when constructing new knowledge and applying skills to demonstrate learning. Allowing students to create apps, games, Web sites, business plans, virtual worlds, and videos can play roles in developing and enhancing this skill.
- **Global Awareness.** Web-based tools and other forms of technology empower students to connect with peers across the globe and develop a better understanding of issues, customs, cultures, architecture, and economics. In a globally connected world, this skill has become sought after by employers whose professions know no geographical bounds.
- **Technological Proficiency.** The importance of this skill goes without saying. The more reliant society becomes on technology, the more we must effectively embed it into the teaching and learning culture to adequately prepare students for the real world.
- **Digital Media Literacy.** Students today to need be given opportunities to create and consume digital content to develop essential literacies. They need to learn how to interpret an array of new messages conveyed through digital media.
- **Digital Responsibility, Citizenship, and Footprints.** When schools routinely integrate technology for learning, they in turn teach their students how to use it appropriately. They

also empower students to develop positive digital footprints when they create content online or share it through social media. These experiences then develop skills that students can and will use to their advantage well beyond their school years.

Appendix C

The Ides of March as Social Media!

The equivalent of social media during the Roman Empire was the interaction in the forum. There, Roman citizens spoke to friends and allies, battled with enemies and "frenemies," and made jokes at one another's expense. Today on Twitter, we engage in the same type of interactions including "Twitter fights," memes, updates, photos, and the use of hashtags to express ourselves and make our views known. We drive the mob and the court of public opinion. Your assignment is to create a Twitter page using your school e-mail for one character from the play of *Julius Caesar*.

REQUIREMENTS

- A header photo using a scene or statue from ancient Rome
- A profile photo using an actual historical image of your character or some kind of clever representation of your character.
- A written profile for your character based on what you find out from quick research and based on what you

find out from the play, *National Geographic* resource, and Plutarch source.

- At least five (one/act) 140-character Tweets in response to material covered in the play. Using the hashtag #JC1WestbrookProject, #JC2WestbrookProject, or #JC4Westbrook project on EACH TWEET. <u>TWEETS without the hashtag will not be given credit.</u>
- At least five 140-character tweets in response to (an) other character(s) using the same hashtag.
- Of the 10 Tweets—one should be created using the MEME Maker at Mozilla Webmaker.
  - Use the following link—you will need to create a free account:
  - https://webmaker.org/en-US/search?type=tags&q=meme
- Of the 10 Tweets at least one should incorporate a photo or image in an intelligent way.
- Earn extra credit for Vine Tweets.
- Make sure content is appropriate for a school assignment (Don't test this!).
- Title your character "CharacterName-NMHS-Your Name."
- (Example: Caesar-NMHS-Joanna (Justins/Viancas/ etc.—use your last initial too.)

What We Are Looking For

<u>Strong Critical Thinking</u>

- Demonstrate an awareness of how the character would react to and understand the events and ideas in the drama
- Demonstrate the complexity and depth of a character's thoughts, beliefs, and actions
- Respond appropriately (in character) to other characters' posts
- Be authentic to the plot and the time. Integrate the history and the play's language and psychology with the

Figure C.1 Assessment Goals

Element	Exemplary 3	Proficient 2	Partially Proficient 1	Unsatisfactory 0	Points
Content	Original Tweets consistently provide new ideas that add value to the discussion. Meme and photo are creative.	Most original Tweets provide new ideas that add value to the discussion. Meme and photo are original and relevant.	A few original Tweets provide new ideas that add value to the discussion. Either meme or photo is missing.	Original Tweets do not provide any new ideas and add no value to the discussion. Neither meme nor photo is present.	__/3
	Tweets are creatively and succinctly written to stimulate dialogue and commentary.	Most Tweets are written to stimulate dialogue and commentary.	A few Tweets are written to stimulate dialogue and commentary.	Tweets are poorly written and do not stimulate dialogue and commentary.	__/3
Frequency	Exceeds the required number of Tweets per week.	Meets the required number of Tweets per week (10).	Falls just short of meeting the required number of Tweets per week (7–9).	Fails to meet the required number of Tweets per week (6 or fewer).	__/3
	Creates and sends Tweets more frequently than required.	Creates and sends Tweets as often as required.	Creates and sends Tweets somewhat less often than required.	Creates and sends Tweets too infrequently to meet the requirements.	__/3

(Continued)

Figure C.1 (Continued)

Element	Exemplary 3	Proficient 2	Partially Proficient 1	Unsatisfactory 0	Points
Mechanics	Writes with no errors in grammar, capitalization, punctuation, and spelling.	Writes with minor errors in grammar, capitalization, punctuation, and spelling.	Writes with major errors in grammar, capitalization, punctuation, and spelling (3 or more errors per Tweet).	Writes with numerous major errors in grammar, capitalization, punctuation, and spelling (more than 5 errors per Tweet).	___/3
Comments and Contributions	Consistently responds to Tweets with positive, respectful, and succinct comments while providing a meaningful addition to the discussion.	Most responses to Tweets are positive and respectful while providing a meaningful addition to the discussion.	Some responses to Tweets are negative and disrespectful and/ or provide little value to the discussion.	Responses to Tweets are negative and disrespectful and provide no value to the discussion.	___/3
	ReTweets are appropriate for the topic and always include the source's Twitter username.	Most reTweets are appropriate for the topic and include the source's Twitter username.	ReTweets are often inappropriate for the topic and fail to include the source's Twitter username.	ReTweets are inappropriate for the topic and show little awareness of the purpose and etiquette of reTweeting.	___/3
Total Points					___/21

modern medium. Do not try to sound too contemporary or Tweet about events that could occur anywhere or at any time. You have 10 things to say, so make them smart.

<u>Characters</u>: Julius Caesar, Brutus, Antony, Cassius, Octavius, Casca, Calpurnia, Portia, Flavius/Marullus, Cinna, any Conspirators, Roman Citizens, Roman soldier from either side.

Comments:

_____

_____

_____

_____

_____

_____

_____

_____

_____

Appendix D

Makerspace Rubric

Figure D.1

	Unsatisfactory	Competent	Proficient	Distinguished
Technique/ Concepts	Work lacks understanding of concepts, materials, and skills.	Work shows some understanding of concepts, materials, and skills.	Work reflects understanding of concepts and materials, as well as use of skills discussed in class.	Work shows a mastery of skills and reflects a deep understanding of concepts and materials.
Habits of Mind	Student passively attempts to fulfill assignment without much thought or exploration of possibilities. Student refuses to explore more than one idea.	Developing exploration of possible solutions and innovative thinking. Student has more than one idea but does not pursue.	Student explores multiple solutions and innovative thinking develops and expands during project.	Consistently displays willingness to try multiple solutions and ask thought-provoking questions, leading to deeper, more distinctive results. Student fully explores multiple ideas and iterations.
Reflection and Understanding	Student shows little awareness of their process. The work does not demonstrate understanding of content.	Student demonstrates some self-awareness. Work shows some understanding of content, but student cannot justify all of their decisions.	Student shows self-awareness. Work demonstrates understanding of content and most decisions are conscious and justified.	Work reflects a deep understanding of the complexities of the content. Every decision is purposeful and thoughtful.

	Unsatisfactory	Competent	Proficient	Distinguished
Craftsmanship	Work is messy and craftsmanship detracts from overall presentation.	Work is somewhat messy and craftsmanship detracts somewhat from overall presentation.	Work is neat and craftsmanship is solid.	Work is impeccable and shows extreme care and thoughtfulness in its craftsmanship.
Responsibility	Frequent illegal absences, tardiness, disrespect for classmates and teacher. Disregard for materials and work such as refusal to clean up or throwing out work.	Student is sometimes illegally absent, tardy, or disrespectful. Must be persuaded to assist in clean up and to take work home.	Student is most often present, on time, and respectful. Usually participates willingly in clean up and takes pride in work.	Student is consistently present, punctual, and respectful of classmates and teacher. Self-directed clean up and ownership of work.
Effort	Work is not completed in a satisfactory manner. Student shows minimal effort. Student does not use class time effectively.	Work complete but it lacks finishing touches or can be improved with a little effort. Student does just enough to meet requirements.	Completed work in an above average manner, yet more could have been done. Student needs to go one step further to achieve excellence.	Completed work with excellence and exceeded teacher expectations. Student exhibited exemplary commitment to the project.

Appendix E

A Series of Articles on Makerspaces From Teacher Librarian Magazine

MAKERSPACES: PART 1 OF MAKING AN EDUCATIONAL MAKERSPACE

Fleming, L., Kurti, S., & Kurti, D. (2014). The philosophy of educational makerspaces: Part 1 of making an educational makerspace. *Teacher Librarian*, *41*(5), 811. Retrieved from http://www.teacherlibrarian.com/2014/06/18/educational-makerspaces/

Synopsis: Educational makerspaces (EMs) and maker education (ME) have the potential to revolutionize the way we approach teaching and learning. ME is a branch of constructivist philosophy that holds that learning is a highly personal endeavor requiring the student to initiate the learning process rather than the teacher. In this philosophy of learning, teachers act as a guide for inquiry-based approaches to the development of knowledge and thinking processes. This article describes the EM and ME movements and offers suggestions that will help students learn with focus on inviting curiosity, inspiring wonder, and encouraging playfulness. Three main takeaway lessons follow: ME inspires deeper learning, EMs are based on student ownership of their learning, and it is not necessary to be a technical expert to start a makerspace in your school or library.

THE ENVIRONMENT AND TOOLS OF GREAT EDUCATIONAL MAKERSPACES: PART 2 OF MAKING AN EDUCATIONAL MAKERSPACE

Fleming, L., Kurti, S., & Kurti, D. (2014). The environment and tools of great educational makerspaces: Part 2 of making an educational makerspace. *Teacher Librarian, 42*(1), 8–12. Retrieved from http://www.teacherlibrarian.com/2014/10/13/educational-makerspaces-pt-2/

Synopsis: Great educational makerspaces (EMs) inspire students to own their learning and deepen their thinking by exploring the world with all their senses. This article explores the look and feel of the environment and the selection of tools of various levels of difficulty to inspire and equip makers to tinker, create, and invent. Innovation is fundamentally an inspired activity, and the right environment has the potential to inspire new thoughts and creative endeavors. Challenges such as time and price, involvement of all stakeholders, and inertia are also addressed.

IMPLEMENTATION OF AN EDUCATIONAL MAKERSPACE: PART 3 OF MAKING AN EDUCATIONAL MAKERSPACE

Fleming, L., Kurti, S., & Kurti, D. (2014). Practical implementation of an educational makerspace: Part 3 of making an educational makerspace. *Teacher Librarian, 42*(2), 20–24. Retrieved from http://www.teacherlibrarian.com/2014/12/17/educational-makerspaces-2/

Synopsis: A culture of innovation in an educational maker-space (EM) arises from student ownership rather than the presence of high-tech tools. Owning the learning experience opens unexplored horizons to students because independent thinkers have the uncanny ability to strike out into uncharted territory whenever limitations block the path. This final part of the series exposes a real-life case study of a makerspace in an average school (New Milford High School in New Jersey) in an average district with results that are anything but average. The article lists seven implementation steps that form a practical and actionable guide to starting an EM either as part of a team or on your own.

References

Alliance for Excellent Education. (2014). Digital Learning Day. Retrieved from http://www.digitallearningday.org/domain/54

An, Y. J., & Reigeluth, C. (2011). Creating technology-enhanced, learner-centered classrooms: K–12 teachers' beliefs, perceptions, barriers, and support needs. *Journal of Digital Learning in Teacher Education, 28*(2), 54–62.

Ball, S. J. (2000). Performativities and fabrications in the education economy: Towards the performative society. *Australian Educational Researcher, 17*(3), 1–24.

Barth, R. S. (1990). *Improving schools from within.* San Francisco: Jossey-Bass.

Benson, P., & Voller, P. (1997). *Autonomy and independence in language learning.* London: Longman.

Berdik, C. (2015). A tiny school in the Ozarks powered a nationally acclaimed turnaround with a mix of technology and trust. *Hechinger Report.* Retrieved from hechingerreport.org/a-tiny-school-in-the-ozarks-powered-a-nationally-acclaimed-turnaround-with-a-mix-of-technology-and-trust/

Bernhardt, V. (2013). *Data analysis for continuous school improvement.* New York: Routledge.

Bevan, B., Petrich, M., & Wilkinson, K. (2014). Tinkering is serious play. *Educational Leadership, 72*(4), 28–33.

Blackwell, L. S., Trzesniewski, K. H., & Dweck, C. S. (2007). Implicit theories of intelligence predict achievement across an adolescent transition: A longitudinal study and an intervention. *Child Development, 78,* 246–263, Study 1.

Blikstein, P. (2013). Digital fabrication and "making" in education: The democratization of invention. In J. Walter-Herrmann & C. Büching (Eds.), *FabLab: Of machines, makers and inventors* (pp. 2–22). Bielefeld, Germany: Transcript.

Branden, N. (1994). *The six pillars of self-esteem.* New York: Bantam.

Caballé, S., Xhafa, F., & Barolli, L. (2010). Using mobile devices to support online collaborative learning, *Mobile Information Systems, 6*(1), 27–47.

Carmody, T. (2012). Google's Sergey Brin: China, SOPA, Facebook threaten the "open web." *Wired.* Retrieved from http://www.wired.com/2012/04/open-web-google-brin/

Center for Digital Education. (2014). Mobility & cloud. Retrieved from http://825d0007e19cfb8330f5-793aa0e2839afbbc4a0b9a463 76ed589.r13.cf1.rackcdn.com/CDE13_SPQ4_V.PDF

Clayton Christensen Institute. (2012). Blended learning model definitions. Retrieved from http://www.christenseninstitute.org/blended-learning-definitions-and-models/

Cristol, D., & Gimbert, B. (2013). Academic achievement in BYOD classrooms. Proceedings from QScience *12th World Conference on Mobile and Contextual Learning.* mLearn, 15.

Cushman, K. (1994). Empowering students: Essential schools' missing link. *Horace, CES National,* 11(1).

D'Avanzo, C. (1996). Three ways to teach ecology labs by inquiry: Guided, open-ended, and teacher collaborative. *The Bulletin of the Ecological Society of America, 77,* 92–93.

Darling-Hammond, L., Zielezinski, M. B., & Goldman, S. (2014). Using technology to support at-risk learning. Retrieved from http://www.all4ed.org/wp-content/uploads/2014/09/UsingTechnology.pdf

Deal, T. E., & Peterson, K. D. (1999). *Shaping school culture: The heart of leadership.* San Francisco: Jossey-Bass.

DeNisco, A. (2014, January). Emerging faces of blended learning. *District Administration,* 32–37.

Duman, B. (2010). Effects of brain-based learning on academic achievement: A sample case of in-class application. *Eurasian Journal of Educational Research, 41,* 91–115. Retrieved from http://new.peoplepeople.org/wp-content/uploads/2012/07/Brain-based-Learning.pdf

Dweck, C. S. (2006). *Mindset: The new psychology of success.* New York: Random House.

Fleming, L. (2015b). *Worlds of making: Best practices for establishing a makerspace for your school.* Thousand Oaks, CA: Corwin.

Fleming, L., Kurti, S., & Kurti, D. (2014). The philosophy of educational makerspaces: Part 1 of making an educational makerspace. *Teacher Librarian, 41*(5), 8–11.

Fleming, L., Kurti, S., & Kurti, D. (2014). The environment and tools of great educational makerspaces: Part 2 of making an educational makerspace. *Teacher Librarian, 42*(1), 8–12.

Fleming, L., Kurti, S., & Kurti, D. (2014). Practical implementation of an educational makerspace: Part 3 of making an educational makerspace. *Teacher Librarian, 42*(2), 20–24.

Fontichiaro, K., & Elkordy, A. (2015). Chart students' growth with digital badges. *International Society for Technology in Education.* Retrieved from http://www.iste.org/explore/articleDetail?articleid=320

Freidman, T. (2013). Can't we do better? *New York Times.* Retrieved from www.nytimes.com/2013/12/08/opinion/sunday/friedman-cant-we-do-better.html?_r=1&

Fulton, K. (2012). Upside down and inside out: Flip your classroom to improve student learning. *Learning & Leading With Technology, 39*(8), 12–17.

Futurelab. (2004). Mobile technologies and learning report. Retrieved from http://archive.futurelab.org.uk/resources/publications-reports-articles/literature-reviews/Literature-Review203

Gerstein, J. (2014). Educator as a maker. Retrieved from usergenerat-ededucation.wordpress.com/2014/06/02/educator-as-a-maker-educator/

Gordon, D. (2011). Remote learning: Technology in rural schools: Making sure students in rural areas get the same quality of educational experience as their counterparts in urban and suburban neighborhoods can be enhanced by the right kind of technology implementation. *THE Journal (Technological Horizons in Education), 38*(9), 18.

Grant, B., & I. Vatnick. (1998). A multi-week inquiry for an undergraduate introductory biology laboratory: Investigating correlations between environmental variables and leaf stomata density. *Journal of College Science Teaching, 28,* 109–112.

Hattie, J. (2012). *Visible learning for teachers: Maximizing impact on learning.* London: Routledge.

Heick, T. (2013). An inquiry framework: 5 levels of student ownership. *TeachThought*. Retrieved from www.teachthought.com/learning/inquiry-framework-levels-student-ownership/

Heick, T. (2014). 6 principles of genius hour in the classroom. *TeachThought*. Retrieved from www.teachthought.com/trends/6-principles-of-genius-hour-in-the-classroom/

Herrington, J., & Kervin, L. (2007). Authentic learning supported by technology: Ten suggestions and cases of integration in classrooms. *Educational Media International, 44*(3), 219–236.

Hidden Curriculum. (2014). In S. Abbott (Ed.), *The glossary of education reform*. Retrieved from edglossary.org/hidden-curriculum

Holec, H. (1981). *Autonomy in foreign language learning*. Oxford, UK: OUP.

Hughes, W. H., & Pickeral, T. (2013). School climate and shared leadership. In T. Dary, & T. Pickeral (Ed.), *School climate practices for implementation and sustainability. A School Climate Practice Brief, Number 1*. New York: National School Climate Center.

Hunter, M. (1982). *Mastery teaching*. El Segundo, CA: TIP.

Jang, H., & Reeve, J. (2005). Engaging students in learning activities: It's not autonomy support or structure, but autonomy support and structure. Unpublished manuscript, University of Wisconsin–Milwaukee.

Jantjies, M., & Joy, M. (2013). Mobile learning through indigenous languages: Learning through a constructivist approach. Proceedings from *12th World Conference on Mobile and Contextual Learning*. Qatar: College of the North Atlantic.

Koehler, M. J., & Mishra, P. (2009). What is technological pedagogical content knowledge? *Contemporary Issues in Technology and Teacher Education, 9*(1), 60–70.

Koehler, M. (2012). TPACK explained. Retrieved from http://www.matt-koehler.com/tpack/tpack-explained/

Koole, M. L. (2009). A model for framing mobile learning. In M. Ally (Ed.), *Mobile learning: Transforming the delivery of education and training* (pp. 25–47). Edmonton, AB: Athabasca University Press.

Kouzes, J. M., & Posner, B. Z. (2007). *The leadership challenge* (4th ed.). San Francisco: Jossey-Bass.

Leithwood, K. A., & Riehl, C. (2003). *What we know about successful school leadership*. Nottingham, England: National College for School Leadership.

Lombardi, M. M. (2007). Authentic learning for the 21st century: An overview. *Educause Learning Initiative.* Retrieved from http://net.educause.edu/ir/library/pdf/ELI3009.pdf

Marlowe, C. (2012). *The effect of the flipped classroom on student achievement and stress.* Retrieved from http://etd.lib.montana.edu/etd/2012/marlowe/MarloweC0812.pdf

Means, B. (2010). Technology and education change: Focus on student learning. *Journal of Research on Technology in Education, 42*(3), 285–307.

Mishra, P., & Koehler, M. (2006). Technological pedagogical content knowledge: A framework for teacher knowledge. *Teachers College Record, 108*(6), 1017–1054.

Murphy, M. (2015). As market surges, schools struggle to find the best tech products. *Hechinger Report.* Retrieved from hechingerreport.org/as-market-surges-schools-struggle-to-find-the-best-tech-products/

Ohlhorst, S. (1995). Successes using open-ended inquiry with college undergraduates and K–12 teachers. Supplement to *Bulletin of the Ecological Society of America, 76*(3, part 3), 371.

Ojalvo, H. E., & Doyne, S. (2011). Five ways to flip your classroom. *New York Times.* Retrieved from http://learning.blogs.nytimes.com/2011/12/08/five-ways-to-flip-yourclassroom-with-the-new-york-times/

Open University. (2013). Innovating Pedagogy Report. Retrieved from http://www.open.ac.uk/personalpages/mike.sharples/Reports/Innovating_Pedagogy_report_2013.pdf

Papert, S. (1993). *Mindstorms: Children, computers, and powerful ideas.* New York: Basic Books.

Perkins, D., & Zimmerman, M. (1995). Empowerment theory, research, and application. *American Journal of Community Psychology, 23,* 569–580.

Project RED. (2015). Retrieved from http://www.projectred.org

Puentedura, R. P. (2012). The SAMR model: Six exemplars. Retrieved from www.hippasus.com/rrpweblog/archives/2012/08/14/SAMR_SixExemplars.pdf

Ravitch, D. (2013). *Reign of error.* New York: Alfred A. Knopf.

Reconnect Learning. (2014). Why digital badges matter. Retrieved from http://www.reconnectlearning.org/why-badges-matter

Reigeluth, C. M. (1996). A new paradigm of ISD? *Educational Technology, 36,* 13–20.

Rule, A. C. (2006). Editorial: The components of authentic learning. *Journal of Authentic Learning, 3*(1), 1–10.

Rycik, J. A. (2012). Building capacity for reform. *American Secondary Education, 40*(3), 80.

Sheninger, E. (2014). *Digital leadership: Changing paradigms for changing times.* Thousand Oaks, CA: Corwin.

Shulman, L.S. (1986). Those who understand: Knowledge growth in teaching. *Educational Researcher, 15*(2), 4–14.

Stewart, L. (2014). Maker movement reinvents education. *Newsweek.* Retrieved from http://www.newsweek.com/2014/09/19/maker-movement-reinvents-education-268739.html

Sundberg, M. D., & Moncada, G. (1994). Creating effective investigative laboratories for undergraduates. *BioScience, 44*(10), 698–704.

TeachThought. (2014). 5 dimensions of critical digital literacy: A framework. Retrieved from http://www.teachthought.com/featured/5-dimensions-of-critical-digital-literacy/

Toppo, G. (2011). Flipped classrooms take advantage of technology. *USA Today.* Retrieved from http://www.usatoday.com/news/education/story/2011-10-06/flipped-classrooms-virtual-teaching/50681482/1

Tough, A. (1971). The adult's learning projects: A fresh approach to theory and practice in adult learning. Toronto, Ontario: Institute for Studies in Education.

Tyre, P. (2012). The writing revolution. *The Atlantic.* Retrieved from www.theatlantic.com/magazine/archive/2012/10/the-writing-revolution/309090/

U.S. Department of Education. (2010). Evaluation of evidence-based practices in online learning: A meta-analysis and review of online learning studies. Retrieved from http://www2.ed.gov/rschstat/eval/tech/evidence-based-practices/finalreport.pdf

Vander Ark, T. (2014). How digital learning is boosting achievement. Retrieved from http://www.gettingsmart.com/2014/03/how-digital-learning-is-boosting-achievement/

Vossoughi, S., Escudé, M., Kong F., & Hooper, P. (2013, October). *Tinkering, learning and equity in the after-school setting.* Paper presented at the Annual FabLearn Conference. Palo Alto, CA: Stanford University.

Wallace Jr., R. C., Engel, D. E., & Mooney, J. E. (1997). *The learning school: A guide to vision-based leadership.* Thousand Oaks, CA: Corwin.

Waters, T., Marzano, R. J., & McNulty, B. (2003). *Balanced leadership: What 30 years of research tells us about the effect of leadership on student achievement.* A working paper.

Yokana, L. (2015). Sample rubric. *Edutopia.* Retrieved from http:// www.edutopia.org/pdfs/blogs/edutopia-yokana-maker-rubric.pdf

Index

A SAGE Company

Helping educators make the greatest impact

CORWIN HAS ONE MISSION: to enhance education through intentional professional learning.

We build long-term relationships with our authors, educators, clients, and associations who partner with us to develop and continuously improve the best evidence-based practices that establish and support lifelong learning.

Learning Forward (formerly National Staff Development Council) is an international association of learning educators committed to one purpose in K–12 education: Every educator engages in effective professional learning every day so every student achieves.